'Preachers we have in abu  have become exceedingly such a day where men and themselves and the attention more highly than the approval of Jesus Christ. I am so thankful that in the midst of the noise of Christian culture, there are still some who are only seeking to point to Jesus Christ. David Harris is such a man. The times that I have heard him minister have always left me hungry for more of Jesus and for the fellowship of the Holy Spirit. I believe that David is a man who is called by God like John the Baptist to declare to the nations, "Behold, the Lamb of God!" As you read *Rescue,* I pray that the Holy Spirit will set your heart on fire with love for Jesus Christ like never before. He deserves all of our love and our highest devotion!'
Lydia Stanley Marrow, Shake The Nations Ministries

'In this awe-inspiring journey, dear friend David Harris takes us down the path of enlightenment, encounter and empowerment through the all-giving source of Life Divine. I believe this written experience will radically transform your life like never before. As you dive into this book, may you be forever branded by the burning love of Jesus Christ our Bridegroom King.'
Brian Guerin, Bridal Glory International

'My wife Tahmar and I have come to know David and his wife Noreen as family. This book is a wonderful testament to the man I've come to know as a friend, and it helps the reader understand the pain behind the pulpit. This is not just David's autobiography, but all of ours.

'We are invited into David's deepest tragedies, losses and triumphs so we can find hope as we journey with Christ to navigate the many estuaries and marshy swamps of our own lives. David has found a hope in Christ that delivered him from drug addiction and the excruciating grief felt with the loss of a beloved father. His journey aids all of us to conclude that time is not the best healer – Jesus is!'

Tomi Arayomi, Tomi Arayomi Ministries

RESCUE

FROM DARKNESS TO LIGHT

DAVID HARRIS

instant
apostle

First published in Great Britain in 2020

Instant Apostle

The Barn
1 Watford House Lane
Watford
Herts
WD17 1BJ

British Library Cataloguing-in-Publication Data

A catalogue record for this book is available from the British Library.

This book and all other Instant Apostle books are available from Instant Apostle:

Website: www.instantapostle.com

Email: info@instantapostle.com

ISBN 978-1-912726-16-5

Printed in Great Britain.

Dedication

First and foremost, I dedicate this book to my all and everything, Jesus Christ. There is none that has loved me as You have. I am forever grateful for Your mercy and caring heart. If it wasn't for You, my life would cease to exist. Today, I live only because You gave Your life for mine and the reason I write is because You captivated my heart with Your tender words. You alone are worthy of every breath I breathe; I will love You forever.

I also dedicate this book to my late father, Samuel Harris. Looking into his eyes I could see the Jesus that I now know today. Though he is physically not here, I am still learning from his life. Up until today, I have yet to meet an earthly man who carried humility as he did; one of the most tender and most loving hearts I have ever known. You will always be my hero; I love you.

Contents

Foreword

*'For God is good – or rather, of all goodness He is
the Fountainhead.'
Athanasius of Alexandria[1]*

I tilted my head back and breathed in the sweet
atmosphere of the still presence of God. David began to
pray, 'Jesus, You are too good to look at.' After he said
these words, I heard nothing else. I was taken into a
consciousness of God's great kindness towards people.
And more personally, His goodness towards me.
Undeserved goodness. Goodness that could only be
wrought by someone far greater than anything mere
humanity is capable of. Such goodness is difficult not only
to accept but to even acknowledge. We tend to pull away
from its grand nature. Most likely because it is a complete
exposing of our utter wickedness and His matchless and
unfathomable love for us. Charles Wesley's words ring
increasingly true:

---

[1] St. Athanasius, *On the Incarnation* (St Vladimir's Seminary
Press, 2007).

> Amazing love, how can it be,
> that Thou my God shouldst die for me? …
> My chains fell off, my heart was free,
> I rose, went forth and followed Thee.[2]

The apostle Paul tells us that His great goodness leads people to repentance (Romans 2:4). Such a goodness is not confined to our initial experience of Him; it is rather stored up for those who fear Him (Psalm 31:19). The psalmist says that it is literally unsearchable (Psalm 145:3). It is so abundant that it cannot be exhausted. For it is inseparable from His wonderful person. This is the reason God showed Moses His goodness when Moses asked to see His glory (Exodus 33:19).

As I read through this volume that David Harris has penned, I felt it to be a wonderful exposition of that sentence he prayed when we sat together in the stillness of God's presence: 'Jesus, You are too good to look at.' Spared from death and having received countless mercies – most of all the rapturous joy of knowing Jesus – we are again and again rescued by such goodness. David's words have been distilled in the presence of the One who holds his heart.

In these days we are in great need of an undimmed love. For as iniquity abounds, the love of many will wax cold. This book will quicken your heart to love Jesus and, even more practically, bring you to let Him rescue you every day. I am glad the book is not named Rescued, for that would fall miserably short of the magnitude of that saving work Jesus performs. He is a daily saviour. A

---

[2] Charles Wesley, 'And Can It Be' (1738).

constant King and an endless romance. For His great rescuing nature not only delivers us from the terrors of the judgement coming against sin, but it is also the satisfaction of His love and the beauty of His reign in our lives. For in this threefold cord we see the rescuing goodness of God in Christ.

I feel a quote from J. I. Packer would be a suitable summary of the love and safety I felt from God while reading this book.

> Guidance, like all God's acts of blessing under the covenant of grace, is a sovereign act. Not merely does God will to guide us in the sense of showing us his way, that we may tread it; he wills also to guide us in the more fundamental sense of ensuring that, whatever happens, whatever mistakes we may make, we shall come safely home. Slippings and strayings there will be, no doubt, but the everlasting arms are beneath us; we shall be caught, rescued, restored. This is God's promise; this is how good he is.[3]

Eric Gilmour
London Gatwick Airport, 26 September 2019
Sonship International

---

[3] J I Packer, *Knowing God* (London: InterVarsity Press, 1993).

Introduction

My entire life I had grown up in a Christian home and although my parents were believers, my heart was far from God. I had experienced what it meant to have religion as part of my life, but it was only through the relationship which God offered to me through His Son, Jesus Christ, that I would truly see my heart transformed.

I began to feel a deep stirring in my heart to write about my journey of how I came to faith in Jesus. I would never have imagined I was able enough to write a book of any sort, but when I heard the Holy Spirit asking me to do it, I knew without a doubt that He would give me the ability to write it. There are already so many great books out there and the last thing I wanted was to write for the sake of writing. In a season of waiting upon God and more recently through voices prophetically confirming what God had spoken to me, I felt a strong leading by the Holy Spirit that this was the period of time in which God wanted me to put my heart onto these pages.

You will come to see the endless possibilities of what God is able to do through the most unlikely situations we face in life. Whether it was loss, or death, redemption from darkness, relational healing, or my call to ministry, I've been through things by the grace of God and it is my honour to share some of those experiences throughout the course of this book. I wouldn't call it a biography – more of an introduction of how I came to know Jesus, the One who totally transformed me and turned my world upside down.

I have shared some of the most personal encounters that I've ever experienced, in which God changed the course of my destiny, and I believe as you read, you too will come into a living experience with Jesus. I have also shared about some of the seasons I went through, which weren't always as easy and straightforward as I would have liked. I have done my best to express my story through vulnerability, in keeping it transparent and honest, so that those of you who may be going through similar issues can see that there is hope and purpose, which can be found in the light of God's presence.

This book is by no means written to reflect a type of religion, but rather its purpose is to show you that there is a God who is deeply in love with you and desires an intimate and personal relationship with humanity. As you read through these pages, I only ask for you to keep your heart open to Jesus; He is looking to touch us far more than we can ever comprehend. This is my story and testimony of going from death to life through the living experience of God Himself. May you come to recognise the grace and goodness of Jesus, to whom I have given my heart; only He can truly satisfy our hearts with a love that cannot be found anywhere else in this life.

For he has rescued us from the dominion of darkness and brought us into the kingdom of the Son he loves.

Colossians 1:13

Chapter One
Lost

Remember your Creator in the days of your youth,
before the days of trouble come and the years
approach when you will say, 'I find no pleasure in
them'
Ecclesiastes 12:1

One of the strangest parts of growing up was always getting the strangest look when I gave my name when introducing myself. I guess back then there were many confused British people who couldn't put a Pakistani together with an English name.

Born in London in 1984, I grew up in a Christian home; both of my parents were from Pakistan. They had immigrated to England and lived in a quiet part of north London. I had three elder siblings: my half-brother and sister, who both lived with their mum not too far from us, and my sister, who grew up in the same house as me. Being the youngest child in the family I was rather spoilt; I was Daddy's boy, so I got what I wanted most of the time. There was also a slightly unusual side to me where I wouldn't talk to any girls apart from my mum and my sister Jessica. It's funny to think that my mum made a complaint to my schoolteacher telling her I had a problem speaking to girls; my teacher explained to her that she was a very lucky mum and that I'd grow out of that phase! It did, however, take the best part of ten years to get past that awkward stage of my life.

My parents raised me with good morals and did their best to set an example of how to lead a good life. They both worked hard to keep our household financially stable and, as I look back, I am thankful that I haven't any bad memories of growing up as a child.

From the very beginning of my life I always had a mischievous side to me. One day we were out shopping as a family. I was around four years old at the time. I'm not sure why, but I thought it would be a good idea to hide behind a curtain in one of the department stores. Once my parents realised I was missing, they alerted the staff and were extremely worried. After searching everywhere, they couldn't find me and by now my mum was left sobbing and my dad terribly distressed. They were on the verge of calling the police when eventually Mum came and stood near to the curtain where I was hiding. I gently reached out, tapped Mum on her back and gave her the surprise of her life. I thought it was funny at the time, but I ended up getting a good telling off, which I rightly deserved.

As a child, there were always many people around me and I was never short of friends. Although my immediate family was relatively small, I grew up in the midst of a large community. It was part of our culture as a family that anyone who was a grown-up automatically became an aunty or uncle. My family was very social – we constantly had people visit our home for dinner and we too would often travel to see our relatives and family friends.

During the school holidays my sister would take care of me while my parents were at work. After finishing my household chores, I would call my mum at work and ask her if I could go outside to play. That was always the best part of my day. I would meet my friends at the back of our flat and we would hang out for hours playing and riding our bikes. Right behind where we lived there was a golf course and sometimes we jumped over the fence and strolled around collecting golf balls. One day, I think I must have collected over twenty balls; I'm not even entirely sure why, but at the time it seemed like a fun thing to do. I never intended to, but I hope I never ruined anyone's game.

As far as faith was concerned, I was christened as a child and on most Sundays we would attend the church near where we lived. I can recall many times when at home we would pray together as a family and Mum would read us stories from the Bible and teach us scriptures.

In my early teenage years, I was confirmed in the Church of England; this is a ritual that takes place once you are old enough to publicly affirm your faith and can begin taking Holy Communion. Though I had gone through a series of Christian teachings, it wasn't something that my heart was given over to. I was just doing it because that's what everyone was meant to do and all the boxes of what religion was meant to look like were being ticked. There was never a moment in which I

21

had any meaningful experience that left a lasting impact on my life. Going to church wasn't the favourite part of my week and I can't say that it ever did anything for me, but in spite of that I still continued to attend based on the faith of my family, as I wasn't really given a choice.

During my late teenage years, I finished my exams at secondary school and I was no longer that strange child who never spoke to girls. By the time I was at college, I became involved in a serious relationship and my life began to take a very different path. I was spending much more time away from home with my friends and once I passed my driving test I was looking for every opportunity to get out of the house.

Though I loved my family, my relationship with them wasn't very open and honest. I would keep myself closed and never confide or share any details about my life on the outside. If I did share anything it was probably a lie anyway, mainly because I thought they would be upset and angry, especially if they knew I was dating someone. Though we were living in England, there were still cultural roots from our Asian background which shaped the way we lived. I found the easiest route was to keep things to myself; even if my parents might have approved, I was convinced they would never understand. It wasn't necessarily bad at home; I was just living out of two very different identities. At home I was trying to act as if everything was normal, whereas on the outside I was completely different. The more time I spent with my friends, the more distant I became with my family. There was never any real transparency on my part, which affected those who loved me the most.

I was hardly going to church any more. The times I did go I found the services to be extremely tiresome; in fact it became a ritual for me to only attend at Christmas and Easter. There was no real motivation, and as far as I was concerned it was a boring place to be and I had better things to do. I'd always give my parents an excuse why I couldn't go and although they weren't very happy about it, they would never force me.

After finishing my course at college, my plan was to go to university to complete a degree in business. I had a dream that one day I would become a successful businessman and desired to become wealthy enough to own several properties and earn a substantial income. As well as my career goals, I was excited about living away from home on campus. I had just about managed to hit the pass mark at college and decided to enrol for a business computing course at Kingston University. It was my first time away from home and it was here that I experienced more freedom than I had before.

From the moment I arrived on campus I was already on the search for the best freshers' parties around. The independence excited me; money wasn't an issue as most students like me were eligible to receive a student loan. On most nights I was going out clubbing and drinking, and soon after that I began smoking cigarettes. One party led to another and I couldn't get enough. If I wasn't drinking to get drunk, I couldn't see the point of it. I was no longer in my previous relationship and so that made going out even more interesting. After most nights out I would wake up with a terrible hangover and would have no energy to even get out of bed, let alone attend my lectures.

After the first few weeks had gone by, I settled into this new lifestyle quite comfortably. By now I had found myself new friends, friends who, like me, enjoyed a good night out. I went from smoking cigarettes to smoking cannabis. At first, I was just trying it out because everyone around me was doing it, but little did I know that I'd soon get hooked on it. I was constantly getting high with my friends and it got to the point where I began to smoke it almost every day, even when I was alone. At the time I would never have thought it was anything serious; in my head I'd justify it as being nowhere near as harmful as cocaine or heroin, but the truth is, I became addicted to it and I was literally getting high at every opportunity. I would carry eye whitener and a good can of deodorant wherever I went so that no one would get suspicious, but I think most people who were around me could see through it. Somewhere in the back of my mind I knew it wasn't the right way of living – it wasn't what my parents had taught me – yet for some reason I believed there wasn't anything wrong in what I was doing. I had become blinded to the reality of what was actually happening.

Most weekends I would go back to my parents' home. I was working part-time at a local retail store and it also gave me the chance to see my family, but even on those weekends I wasn't at home much. I had become so accustomed to going out that I would make time to meet with my friends who lived nearby and as soon as I had the chance, I was out of the house again.

By the end of my first year at university I had only attended a handful of lectures. I was nowhere near a position of passing, so I decided to go back the next year to restart on another course. I had it all planned out in my head, that I would get my act together and make sure that I would pass this time around; failing wasn't going to be an option. But the year started and my short-lived dream was over before it had even begun. Right from the beginning it was a repeat of my first year – only worse. Again, I failed to attend my lectures and I continued to live a life that was giving me the pleasures I desired. There were moments that I'd wonder what on earth I was doing and how was I going to tell my family where the last two years of my life had gone, but the thoughts would quickly evaporate as I continued to keep myself busy.

From getting drunk to getting high, wanting to have status and popularity, sleeping around with girls and spending money that wasn't mine, from being involved in fights and being arrested for disruptive behaviour – what did it matter? The satisfaction of my rebellion outweighed the disappointments. As I came to the end of the second year, I knew this time I wouldn't be coming back.

I moved back home, and it was time to face my family. I could sense they knew I wasn't on the right path; however, they never used it against me. Soon after I had returned, they sat me down and I remember my mum asking me, 'What are you going to do with your life?'

I expected them to be angry, but they weren't; it was an unusually calm situation. I was honest for once; I told them that I wanted to leave university and quit studying. I wanted to continue working part-time and in the meantime look for something more permanent. I could tell they were hurting on the inside – all those years they had invested in my life, to see me ruining it – but somehow they held it together. I couldn't imagine what they were feeling, seeing me the way I was, but in the midst of disappointment I could almost sense that they still had hope in me.

Looking back over all those years I can only describe it as a roller coaster of a journey. I had spent my entire life studying, to eventually come out as a failure with no relevant qualifications. Most of my friends who I knew during my time at university had continued to study and earn their degrees. Here I was, left in the mess that I had created for myself. Despite having grown up in a home that wasn't broken and having parents who taught me good morals, ultimately I was the one who was responsible for my own destiny through the choices and decisions I had made.

After leaving university I felt as if my mind wasn't in its right place; my emotions had become numb (smoking all that cannabis was partly to blame for that). Somewhere on the inside I knew I needed to sort myself out, but it was something that could always wait until another day. Other than satisfying my personal desires, there was no true meaningful purpose to my life.

As selfish as it may sound, I became content living for what I found pleased me the most. Whether it was good or bad it did not matter, and I wasn't at all concerned that others would get hurt by the way I chose to live.

Chapter Two
Death

Just as people are destined to die once, and after
that to face judgment ...
Hebrews 9:27

My lifestyle hadn't ¯changed much since leaving university; the only difference was that it was now all happening much closer to home. While living away, I had got myself into a lot of debt and although I was working part-time, I was more concerned about having enough money so I could continue to feed my own desires, rather than clear the money that I owed.

On most weekends I was out partying with my friends, getting high and chasing girls. Sometimes I would get back home so late that it was actually the early hours of the morning. I would often hear Mum quietly praying in her bedroom, while I was tiptoeing back into my own room. She would always tell me that she couldn't sleep until she knew I was safely home, and would stay up praying for me. This had become the normal way of living for me. I seemed not to care about those who were around me, those who were the nearest and those who loved me.

While working part-time I was also searching for potential career opportunities. Fortunately for me, my brother-in-law had his own recruitment firm. He was well connected and managed to get me an interview at an insurance company in the City. Little did I know that I would be offered the job, and working in this sector would become my career for the next eleven years.

I now had a full-time job, which paid much more than I was used to. The only issue was, the more money I had, the more I would love to spend. As well as wasting money on my addictive lifestyle, I developed a new interest in performance cars and had purchased one for myself. I would spend into the thousands customising and upgrading parts. There were many nights I was racing around town with a group of friends who all had fast cars. We would drive at ridiculously high speeds for hours during the night. I'm surprised I never got into any major accidents and am alive to tell my story today. On numerous occasions I was pulled over by the police for speeding, but I was fortunate not to have got into any serious trouble other than having penalty points placed on my licence.

One day I was travelling with a friend to a garage near Oxford where I was having some work done on my car. On the journey back home, I started to smell petrol, so we pulled up into a car park at a fast-food drive-through near west London. I popped open the bonnet of my car and noticed the fuel injectors were leaking. This could have potentially set my car on fire, but thankfully it never got to that point.

While I was figuring out what to do, I heard a car accelerating at high speed. As I turned to look, I saw two cars racing each other – both coming in my direction. The first car flew past me, but the second car spun out of control. It eventually smashed into a tree, catapulted fifteen feet into the air, and then came crashing back down to the ground.

My friend who was with me told me to go over and see if everyone was OK. As I made my way towards the crash, it all seemed to happen in slow motion; the closer I got, the more I realised how bad the situation was. I had never seen anything like it before. There were two people inside, barely conscious, and there was blood everywhere. I kneeled down to see if the driver was OK. He acknowledged me, but couldn't say anything. I then looked over to the passenger; he seemed a lot worse than the driver, but he was still awake and still breathing. The car was caved in at the front and it looked as if their legs had been crushed. Within minutes the scene was flooded with ambulance crew and police, who sealed off the perimeter. I was told by the police I needed to stay to give a witness statement. I couldn't help but lean over to see what was happening and hoped it was all going to be OK. As I watched, I could see the passenger choke and cough up blood. A paramedic rushed over with an oxygen mask, but I could just sense in that moment he had taken his last breath. I went home that night thinking about what had happened over and over again.

Months later I was interviewed by the police to give my statement and I was told the very thing I felt the night I was there – the passenger had died at the scene. He was just twenty-one; a student from India who had come to study in the UK. The situation couldn't have been any more tragic.

Things continued as usual for me, but there were definitely times it made me think how short life was. Yet it never really sank in, or changed the way I valued life.

It was towards the end of 2007 that my dad began to develop a cough. Being a former boxer who had competed in the Olympics, Dad was physically fit and strong; even though he was in his early seventies he was more active than anyone else I knew. He went to the doctor, but the cough persisted and he was sent for further tests. At the time it never felt like it was serious or life-threatening, but by the beginning of 2008 the situation became much worse, and to help with his breathing my dad constantly carried a supply of oxygen wherever he went. It was not long afterwards that we received the unexpected news that no person ever wishes to hear – Dad was diagnosed with pulmonary fibrosis, a life-debilitating disease. He was told he had only six months to live.

I couldn't believe what I was hearing; I could not grasp the thought of my dad not being with us any more. As a family it was heartbreaking for all of us. My dad was someone that always went out of his way to make sure I was happy; he was someone who could walk into a room and light up the atmosphere with his smile. He never had anything negative to say, was always humble, kind and softly spoken; I never knew anyone like him. Even during the darker days of my life when my mum would be upset with me, he would always give her hope that one day I would get better.

Over the course of the next few months my dad's health began to deteriorate. I would like to say I was there to take care of him, but the truth is that I was far from being the son I needed to be. My mum and sister were the ones who were really there for him; even my elder brother and sister, who were both married, gave more support than I did. The only way I knew how to deal with things was to continue to live life as normal. Within myself I'd always think the situation was just going to get better. I felt the more I kept myself busy, the less I would have to think about it. I was still getting high most days and I continued to go out with my friends whenever I had the chance. On the outside I was trying to keep it together, but there were many moments that the reality of what was happening crept up on me and I would burst out crying as I thought about losing my dad. Friends and family would give their support, but I would feel so empty and alone on the inside.

As the days went on my dad became weaker. The nights were the most difficult. The machine that supplied oxygen was extremely noisy, and someone had to constantly be near Dad throughout the night in case the tubes going up into his nostrils came loose – this could have been fatal for him. My mum and sister would usually take it in turns, although there were a handful of times I helped too.

To help me sleep, I would usually have a smoke in the garden before getting into bed. One night, while looking up at the stars, I started talking aloud to God. I wasn't someone who had 'faith', but I always felt there was a God that existed. For some reason, talking to Him felt like the right thing to do. I wouldn't say much: simple things like 'I trust you, I'm not angry and I believe you will always do what is right'. It never made sense to me why I did this, but I felt Someone was listening and it gave me peace on the inside.

More than six months had passed and my dad was still with us. Even though his health had deteriorated and worsened, he would still manage to put on a brave face. Sometimes ministers we knew from different denominations and friends from church would visit our home to pray for Dad. Most of the time I stayed in my room, but I remember hearing the prayers as my family stood in faith for his healing. Even in the moments when the pain became unbearable and Dad would gasp for breath, I remember him saying 'sweet Jesus, have mercy upon me'. Though he wasn't very mobile and needed to be pushed around in a wheelchair, he never gave up attending church on Sundays. He always wanted to help take up the offering and spend time worshipping God with his church family. If there was anything that I learned, it was that even in the most trying time of Dad's life, he wanted to stay committed and faithful to God.

Nine months had now passed since my dad was first diagnosed and he was eventually taken into a hospice. On 17th October 2008, my dad moved on from this life to another. No words could express the loss and sorrow in my heart. Though my relationship with him had faded in the latter years, I loved him deeply. It was the biggest loss I had faced in my entire life.

Experiencing these traumatic tragedies was a lot to get my head around; so much had happened in such a short space of time and it was difficult to take it all in. I was emotionally stretched and there were countless thoughts of trying to understand what had taken place, but with no real explanation. This was the toughest season of my life, but no one could predict what was to come next.

It was not long afterwards that I was about to experience some of my most life-changing moments.

Chapter Three
Rescue

For he has rescued us from the dominion of darkness and brought us into the kingdom of the Son he loves, in whom we have redemption, the forgiveness of sins.
Colossians 1:13-14

It wasn't easy letting go of my dad. You often hear the saying, 'You don't know what you've got until it's gone.' This describes what I was going through. I wasn't there much during his last years, but that didn't change the fact that I loved him and missed having him with us. He was always going to be my dad. There were moments I would feel my heart ache with a deep sorrow. I wished I could turn back the clock and spend more time with him. Though the process of grieving was a painful experience, there were moments in which I felt an unusual peace that would rest on the inside of me. It gave me some kind of assurance that Dad was free from suffering and in a better place.

After going through the ordeal of losing my dad, I began wanting to spend more time at home with my family. We were stronger together and I began to recognise the value and worth of family again. Being the only male at home, I felt the need to take more responsibility and be there to support them. There were definitely some positive changes that followed. I had quit smoking cigarettes the same week that my dad had passed away, and I wasn't going out as much. I even started attending church again; at the time it felt like the right thing to do and I guess it made part of me feel better about myself.

Though I was beginning to find my place more at home, my old way of living was very present. I would still find the time to be out partying and drinking and although I had stopped smoking cigarettes, I was still getting high on cannabis. You could say that everything had become more balanced, and I guess I never felt so bad if things were being done in moderation. Things may have seemed OK, but I was still living a very double life.

Despite all of that, there were moments I was alone in my room where I would begin to have thoughts which made me question what life was all about. What was the purpose of my existence and the true meaning of everything that surrounded me? After witnessing the death of the young student in the car accident and with the loss of my dad, deep down within me there lingered a list of unanswered questions.

Before going to sleep, I would often think: what would it feel like if I never woke up the next day, or what if I was to die, would I cease to exist? Would I cease to feel? And where would I be? I could never come to a conclusion; I just knew there was more to life than meets the eye and I was curious to know what that was. In some way it was as if I had connected with my spiritual side. I couldn't fathom death being the end of my life and so the question remained: where do we go from here?

I even came to the point where I researched the concept and beliefs of other religions, but nothing seemed to make sense. On top of all that, my sister thought it would be a good idea to hold a weekly Christian youth meeting at our home. I would sit in and try to understand from a biblical perspective the answers to my deep thoughts. We had numerous discussions and it was definitely a mind-opener to see the possibilities of who God could be. I began to understand more about the Christian faith than I had ever done before. I was now going to church every week and was able to grasp more of the truths that the Bible taught. However, I couldn't help but feel an unrestful and empty void on the inside.

It was 12th April 2009. I had attended church with my family for the annual Easter Sunday service. It was nothing out of the ordinary, apart from there being a lot more people compared with a normal Sunday. It was also a good time to catch up with some friends who would only turn up during these times of the year. We enjoyed a good meal at the end with everyone and it was coming close to evening, so we made our way back home.

After we had arrived, I went up to my bedroom and got myself ready to lie down. My mum and sister were both in their own bedrooms and I remember it being really quiet and still. I got into my bed and switched on the television; there was always a good film to watch during Easter, so I began to flick through the channels to see what

I could find. After browsing for a while I came across Mel Gibson's film, *The Passion of the Christ*. I had already watched this film at the cinema several years before; nevertheless, I felt a pull on my heart to watch it again.

During the film there came a scene in which Jesus was hanging on the cross: His arms were stretched out, hands pierced with nails, a crown of thorns pressed upon His head, blood dripping, and wounds all over His body that made Him unrecognisable. The acting was persuasive, but in that moment something occurred to me that I had never truly grasped before. I began to recognise Jesus as a real living person, the Son of God who walked this very earth. The film continued, but my mind was fixed on the scene where Jesus hung, dying on the cross.

In that instant I sensed the atmosphere in my room tangibly shift and I began to feel a weighty presence surrounding me. My entire life I had been labelled as a Christian, but only now did I begin to understand how real God was and how far I was from Him. I saw my life flash before my eyes and in it I could see no good. I had never thought that I was a bad person who deserved to go to hell, but right there before me I could see the corruptness of my heart and how broken I truly was. When I realised how guilty I was before Him, I felt my heart being crushed on the inside; it was like a wrench turning within me. The magnitude of my sin became evident and I was deeply convicted.

I had never known there to be a God that existed in this way and all of a sudden I could sense Him so near. By now my body was trembling, my heart was beating faster than normal and tears were uncontrollably flowing from my eyes. I kept having the repeated thought going through my head: I'm the one who deserves to be crucified on that tree, but Jesus chose to be there in my place. The thought of Jesus dying for me was breaking my heart.

As I became convicted of my sinful self, I began to feel God's heart, filled with endless love, pour into me. The more I realised how deserving I was of death, the more I felt His love come like waves crashing over my heart. This was love like I had never known before, unexplainable and yet undeniable.

> For God so loved the world that he gave his one
> and only Son, that whoever believes in him shall
> not perish but have eternal life.
> *John 3:16*

My soul naked with my sin exposed, nowhere to hide, helpless and weak – there I sat, knowing I had a decision to make. My mind could not fathom His love towards me, but my heart was ready and open to receive all that He was. Sobbing like a baby with my hands open before me, I spoke these simple few words: 'I surrender my all to You, Jesus. I give my life to follow You.' In that moment I felt Him reach into my being. He came with mercy, He came with compassion and He came with forgiveness, but more than anything, He came as a sacrifice to die for me. As I laid my life down before Him, I felt His blood cleanse and wash me from my sin and my past. I knew in that instant something had changed inside me. I was a different person; I could feel Jesus in my heart and sense His peace. Although I had gone to church for most of my life, it was only now that I could make sense of anything.

What took place in my bedroom that night had changed everything. Jesus had given me a new beginning and a new heart. I had gone from death to life and the void inside me was filled with the love of God. Jesus, my Saviour, came and rescued me. His words had come alive to my heart and now I finally knew what it meant when Jesus said, 'I am the way and the truth and the life. No one comes to the Father except through me' (John 14:6).

The next morning I didn't dance or scream, or jump on the roof and shout to tell the world about Jesus; in fact I didn't even feel the need to tell my mum or sister! It was an intimate and sacred moment that had taken place, a divine love exchange between me and God. He was with me and that was all that mattered.

I was overcome by the reality that God Himself, the creator of the heavens and earth, desired to have a personal relationship with me. I was excited that I could now walk this life with Him. As I spent more time reading the Bible and praying, the way in which I viewed the world began to change. I was beginning to perceive things through His heart and not mine. I had a new value and respect for those around me. I began to see people as God's creation, those that He died for and loved.

Things that I previously desired also began to change. Some habits died instantly, the moment I surrendered my life to Jesus, but some changed through a process of time. I would love to say I was completely free from living a life of addiction, but the truth is there was a lot that God still needed to work on in my heart. I felt like a new person on the inside, but although I knew that I was forgiven and cleansed from my sinful nature, the way I was living told a different story. I was still bound in certain parts of my life, I was still getting high and I found it acceptable to occasionally get drunk, so clearly there were areas in which I needed freedom.

There were many scriptures that would speak to me about the way I was living, in particular in the book of Romans where it says, 'Do not conform to the pattern of this world, but be transformed by the renewing of your mind' (Romans 12:2). As I spent time in prayer and let His Word sink into me, I became conscious of His presence. I got to know Jesus as one who had real feelings and one who had a heart. This is where real transformation would take place. Why would I want to hurt the One that I loved? Even more so, the One that loved me and gave His life for me? If sin was the thing that separated us, then why choose to live in it? During that same year I was taken on a journey where I experienced deep convictions, not by disobeying rules, but by experiencing His love for me.

On my twenty-fifth birthday, just a few months after surrendering my life to Jesus, I decided to hire a private hall to gather some friends and family to celebrate. I thought having a few alcoholic drinks wouldn't hurt anyone, but by the end of the night I was a little drunk. The next morning when I woke up, I could feel the Holy Spirit convict my heart. More than feeling bad about what I had done, I could feel I had hurt the One who loved me by choosing to sin against Him. I literally rolled out of my bed and onto my knees and wept before God.

It was His Word coming alive and His continual speaking that brought true liberation in the things that once bound me. At one point I had even taken all my secular music filled with foul language and thrown away hundreds of pounds worth of CDs. The music wasn't what

Jesus represented and there was nothing in it that was pleasing to Him, so why keep it? In this season I experienced Jesus as my faithful deliverer who never gave up on me; my mess was the perfect place for Him to come and sort out, to make right.

My life now held a purpose which I could never see before – it was my God-given destiny to walk in fellowship with Jesus. He was not someone who was sitting far away on a distant throne; He was nearer to me than my breath. He had given me His Holy Spirit to live inside me, and wherever I went, He was right there with me. As time went on, my family could see the change in my lifestyle; they noticed I was walking a different path from before, a path with God, and this was a blessing for all of us.

As I have said before, I grew up in a good home with a loving family, just like the prodigal son who we read about in Luke 15. It wasn't that I strayed because of some childhood hurt that left me broken; I had everything this world could offer and was still empty on the inside. Until I recognised the love of my heavenly Father, I was as lost as anyone else. Jesus was a real person to be known intimately. He wasn't a doctrine or a theology, He wasn't a denomination, He wasn't a good story to read about or a great historical figure – He was my resurrected Saviour who took me from death into eternal life. He is still that same Jesus today. He comes to heal the broken-hearted and set prisoners free.[4]

---

[4] See Luke 4:18-19 (NKJV).

Chapter Four
Transition

There is a time for everything, and a season for
every activity under the heavens.
Ecclesiastes 3:1

What a beautiful reality it became that I could know Jesus intimately, and have a relationship with Him; in fact, He was so near and approachable that I could call Him my friend. In the midst of nearly 7 billion people who exist on planet Earth, I got to know Him personally! Just the thought of it was overwhelming. It was more than just the privilege of knowing Him; it was the vast truth that God Himself desired to have a relationship with me. Throughout my entire life I had never known what my true purpose was, but now that I knew, I wanted to take hold of it with all that I had. God would continually reveal His love to my heart, and as I drew closer to Him, the more I fell in love with Him.

Nearly a year had passed since I had surrendered my life to Jesus. I couldn't believe how much had changed in such a short time and it was unbelievable to think what life had looked like not that long ago. During this season I was still working in insurance, but now it was about more than just earning an income and gaining a successful career. I got to do life with Jesus and that brought joy and purpose. I could live in conversation with Him, whether I was sitting on the train or at my desk at work – throughout every moment, Jesus was with me.

What He had done for me, I knew He could do for anyone else. It wouldn't seem fair to keep this treasure to myself. I wanted everyone to experience the same Jesus that set me free and gave me this new life. His blood was shed for this very reason, that 'all people' might be saved and 'come to a knowledge of the truth' (1 Timothy 2:4). If you were with me at any point during that time, I am certain by the end of our conversation I would have been talking about Jesus and what He has done for us. The purest and truest evangelism was found when I allowed the overflow of my relationship with God to touch others.

There came many occasions where I would still hang out with my unsaved friends and although I wouldn't be getting high or drunk, it gave me the opportunity to share the love of Jesus with them. They were happy that I'd found my purpose in life, but most of them were not prepared to surrender their hearts to Jesus. Even today, many of them are in the same dark places they were in all those years ago, but I still believe there is hope for them as there was for me when I was also lost.

As time went on, I wouldn't hear from them as much as I used to; many of them would make their plans without me and eventually I wouldn't hear from them at all. I only had one Christian friend; his name was Nizam, and we had known each other from my college years. Nizam gave his life to Jesus a few years before me, but we lived a fair distance away from each other and wouldn't get to meet up much. I must admit, during this season I felt extremely lonely. I would even cry out to Jesus because I couldn't understand why my friends were no longer there for me. I remember the Holy Spirit would remind me that Jesus also had a lonely journey; even the disciples who were closest to Him were the very ones who would leave His side when the time came for Him to die. This brought great comfort to my heart and although this season of being lonely was challenging, the challenges became precious moments where Jesus would invite me to draw closer to Him.

In these times of being alone, God would pour out His love on the inside of me and all the expectations I had of the world on the outside would break. Over time, I began to realise that having Jesus was more than anything this world could give me. Jesus was enough to satisfy the depths of my being and He was teaching me that I could live in dependency on Him. As my relationship with Him developed, I became increasingly aware of His presence in my daily life. Prayer wasn't just some ritual or religious duty; it was a place of communion and friendship between me and Jesus. The more I opened the Scriptures and spent time with Him, the more Jesus would unveil to my heart who He was.

I also continued to attend the local church. With my dad not around any more, it was nice to go together as a family – and at the time, it felt like the right place to be. However, I began to find it difficult to 'connect' with the services. This began to make me feel increasingly frustrated. Still, it was never my intention to leave or give up going to church. I knew that God had placed me there for a reason and I wanted to stay faithful to Him. My heart's desire was to make room for the Holy Spirit and see lives encounter Jesus, but to me it felt that the presence of God was taking second place to culture, tradition and church programmes. Not to say that any of those things are particularly wrong, but they are not to be preferred above the love and passion for His presence.

Eventually it came to the point where, as a family, we felt that it was the right decision for us to move on. Within a short time I began to see many relationships that I was part of dissolve. Those that I considered as my closest friends were now the most distant and those at church that were as near as family became strangers. Although Jesus called me to love selflessly, not everyone was going to be my best friend! It was the same with Jesus when He walked the earth.

Jesus never told me that following Him would be easy, but He did promise that He would never leave me when things got hard.[5] His presence was able to outweigh the burden of the trials and challenges I faced. Throughout these difficult seasons, the Holy Spirit was taking perfect care of me. He was working all things for my good[6] and His peace would continually strengthen my heart.

It wasn't long after leaving that a family friend invited me for a weekend retreat that his church was hosting during Easter. At first, I wasn't entirely sure if I wanted to go. I had visited his church and felt uncomfortable with

---

[5] See Matthew 28:20.

[6] See Romans 8:28.

everyone raising their hands during worship, and praying out aloud. This type of environment was unfamiliar to me; it was different to the way I thought of 'church', and what it was meant to look like.

However, around the same time, one of my younger cousins was battling with addictions, similar to what I had faced not that long ago, and his mum asked me to keep an eye on him as she was extremely concerned. Taking the circumstances on board, I gave in and thought if I took my cousin with me, it could be a great opportunity for him to meet with Jesus – and that's exactly what happened. Throughout our time at the retreat we both ended up having some powerful encounters with God. At the end of one of the sessions my cousin asked me to go outside with him, and he took his bag of cannabis and emptied it out on the ground. God had deeply touched his heart and he wanted to surrender his all to Jesus. As for me, by the end of the retreat I had experienced what it meant to be part of God's family in a way I had not known before. Everyone I met seemed to be in love with the same Jesus that I loved and suddenly it was no longer a strange environment that made me feel awkward; in fact, I was now in a position of lifting my own hands, praising Jesus with everyone else – it's amazing how God can turn things around! It was so refreshing to fellowship with other believers and by the end of the retreat, I felt a strong leading in my heart to continue in fellowship with those that I met and so I began to attend their regular services in London.

Church was no longer just a building that I visited once a week; it was somewhere I could experience the presence of God and was a place that I could call my family. The best part of it all was that my mum and sister were also regularly attending.

Not long after I joined the church, I began to develop a good relationship with one of the pastors and was put forward for a leadership programme. Within a few months I was commissioned as one of the leaders and began to take on several responsibilities. Over the next few years I helped lead the youth ministry, as well as being involved in several evangelistic projects. It was a humbling experience, being given the opportunity to pour into many lives and see hearts touched by Jesus. Whether I was given the opportunity to teach or whether I was stacking up chairs at the end of a service, I learned that in all things I could align my heart towards Jesus and do it unto Him.

Not long after joining that church, my friend Nizam invited me over to his house for a Bible study. It was always great to catch up and fellowship together, as we didn't get to see each other often. That day we looked at several scriptures that focused on the work of the Holy Spirit, specifically instances where people spoke in tongues[7] following the infilling of the Spirit. We could see that throughout the scriptures there were believers who received the gift by the laying on of hands.[8] What came as a surprise was at the end Nizam asked if he could lay hands on me and pray for me to receive this supernatural prayer language that God desired to give to me. Nizam

---

[7] See for example 1 Corinthians 14:2. Tongues is a prayer language given by the Spirit of God to edify believers, and to worship God. The language is usually unknown.
[8] See for example Acts 19:6.

went on to tell me he had recently been filled with the Holy Spirit while at a leadership course and received the gift of tongues. While at this course he was given 'homework', to lay hands on somebody else to also receive this gift – apparently that somebody was me! I was caught off guard. However, I was open to receive anything in that moment that God had for me. As Nizam began to pray, I didn't feel anything and I didn't really know what to do, but as he continued to pray, by faith I opened my mouth and began to speak in an unknown tongue. It didn't make sense in my head; at first it sounded like a baby babbling, but as I carried on it was as if a river deep within me had sprung open.

The humorous side to it was that while we were praying, Nizam's dad, who was an unbeliever, walked into the room and stood there watching us pray for each other while we were on our knees. I can't imagine what was going through his mind, but he had the most intriguing expression on his face. It makes me laugh every time I think of it.

This experience still remains a precious heavenly moment which has never left me, and I've continued to pray in tongues ever since, and feel my walk with God has been deepened through my communion with Him.

In the same year I was convicted in my heart to have a water baptism. My family always believed that once we were christened as children another baptism wasn't necessary, but as we studied the scriptures together, I knew I had to make my own decision in obedience to what Jesus taught us in Matthew 28:19-20. Baptism, being fully immersed under water, was a symbolic picture of my life: identifying with the death, burial and resurrection of

Jesus, it was an outward testimony of what God had done on the inside of me, and an act of love to express that my life belonged to Him: 'If you love me, keep my commands' (John 14:15).

On 27th November 2010, it was with so much joy that my mum, my sister and I were all water baptised. It was a holy moment that I shared with the Holy Spirit and I cannot express the overwhelming feeling of happiness that filled my heart and how thankful I was that Jesus made it all happen, not just for me, but for my family too.

More than eighteen months had passed since I had given my heart to Jesus, and He had already done so much, but I knew this was just the beginning. God hadn't just saved me from hell to get to heaven, He saved me for Him. There was so much more of Jesus that I wanted in my life. There was a hunger inside me – I wanted to know Him more intimately. It wasn't going to end with church, it wasn't going to end by praying in tongues and it wasn't going to end in being baptised. I began to understand that the encounter wasn't something that just happened when I first gave my life to follow Jesus; it was rather a continual invitation to come to Jesus and experience Him daily.

Chapter Five
Union

I have given them the glory that you gave me, that
they may be one as we are one — I in them and
you in me — so that they may be brought to
complete unity.
John 17:22-23a

When God created the world we live in today, it was always His intention to live in close, intimate fellowship with humanity. In the Garden of Eden, we read that Adam heard the sound of God walking 'in the cool of the day' (Genesis 3:8). What a beautiful reality it must have been to live in such close proximity with God to the extent you could hear the sound of His very footsteps. Can you imagine how glorious it must have been to live in unbroken fellowship with God, in such nearness to Him? Before sin entered into the world, humanity lived in perfect harmony with God in a perfect relationship. Unhindered, free of guilt and shame, both God and humans lived in divine intimacy, sharing love and delighting in one another. This was God's desire from the very beginning. 'We love because he first loved us' (1 John 4:19).

Although our fellowship with God was damaged because of sin, Jesus came to restore our broken relationship. When Jesus sacrificially died on the cross, not only did He pay the penalty for our sin so we could receive eternal life, but He made a way for us to be reunited with Him, the One who is life Himself. Through the indwelling of the Holy Spirit on receiving Jesus, God has once again given every believer the ability to sense the nearness of His presence. God's desire is to bring humanity into a deeper awareness of Himself and His heart beats for us to know Him intimately. The relationship which was lost through the disobedience of Adam was finally restored through the obedience of Jesus.

> And being found in appearance as a man, he
> humbled himself by becoming obedient to death
> – even death on a cross!
> *Philippians 2:8*

In the book of John, Jesus Himself prayed that we would become one with Him, just as He was one with the Father.[9] Our union with Jesus is connected to our relationship with Him and it is only through our union with Him that we can now live, 'For in him we live and move and have our being' (Acts 17:28). One of the definitions of union states: 'When the union of two or

---

more things occurs, they are joined together and become one thing.'[10]

I firmly believed that in living a life yielded unto Jesus, I could also live in this divine spiritual union with Him. It was more than just a truth; it was now a reality. Paul in the book of Galatians said, 'I no longer live, but Christ lives in me'[11] – this was the very life that I could now also live by placing my faith in Jesus; one where everything was led by Jesus. It was in my union with Him that my true purpose and identity were found; it was in my union with Jesus where I found my belonging. I was learning that as I lived my life through continual surrender to Him, I would experience true freedom and here God could fulfil His word in my life.

During these earlier years of my walk with Jesus I began to recognise the value and worth of simple faith. It was never God's intention that my journey with Him be complicated. On the contrary, it was having childlike faith that gave Him the rightful place as Father in my life; His only requirement was to simply believe. It was having the faith to believe that 'without You, God, I can do nothing'.[12] Rather than trying to do things in my own strength and ability, to be childlike was to be someone that could live in dependency on God. As I began to see Him this way, I recognised I could trust Him with every part of my being. Just as children are dependent upon their parents, so it could be with Jesus. I knew God was always there for me,

---

[10] https://www.collinsdictionary.com/dictionary/english/union (accessed 3rd August 2019).

[11] Galatians 2:20.

[12] See John 15:5.

He was my Father and I could place my trust in His words. To be childlike before God removed every barrier and limitation to what He was able to accomplish through my life.

> See what great love the Father has lavished on us, that we should be called children of God! And that is what we are!
> *1 John 3:1*

Although I had a daily routine, it was so much more than just the mundane activities this life would have to offer. It was now an intimate walk with Jesus, filled with adventure and excitement. Getting to do life with Jesus was not something I could take lightly. To know He was there in every moment made every breath worth breathing and life worth living. I could place my trust in His Word and believe that He knew what was best for me. In His presence I found all that I ever needed to satisfy the depths of my heart. Where there was once a fear and expectation of having to become something in this world, there was now a certainty of knowing that having Jesus was more than anything this life could ever give to me.

I remember on many occasions I would read the Scriptures to increase my knowledge of the Bible, but I felt a difference when I simply read with the motive of wanting to draw closer to Jesus. It went from just reading a good story, to actually experiencing who He was in His words. As I spent time with Him in prayer and reading the Scriptures, I could feel Him change the desires of my own heart with the desires of His. The Holy Spirit would lift the lifeless black ink off the pages and breathe them upon my heart, and it felt like Jesus was kissing me on the inside with His own words. When the Scriptures came alive in this way, I began to perceive things differently: this is where He would mould my heart with His tender words. The Bible went from being a book to being God's love letter to me.

Throughout the Scriptures there is a constant picture which relates to Jesus as the Bridegroom and the Church as His bride.[13] In the Old Testament, God's chosen nation, Israel, is referred to as His wife,[14] and in the New Testament the same analogy is given in reference to the Church. The purpose of marriage between man and woman was always intended to represent the ultimate spiritual marriage between God and His creation. There will come a day when the Church is united with Jesus the Bridegroom.[15] However, until that day, it is the joy of His people to remain faithful to Him. Bridal love for Jesus places Him above everything else, just as He put humanity first when He chose to lay down His own life for the bride that He so desired.[16] Bridal intimacy has only one motive, loving Jesus. It burns with a desire to be with Him and live for Him. It is best summed up in the greatest commandment of all, 'Love the Lord your God with all your heart and with all your soul and with all your mind and with all your strength' (Mark 12:30).

---

[13] See for example Mark 2:19-20 where Jesus is depicted as the Bridegroom.

[14] See Isaiah 54:5-6.

[15] See Revelation 21:2.

[16] See Ephesians 5:25.

There was no limit to my daily interaction with Him. Jesus was after more than just worship on a Sunday morning; He desired a song that would keep on singing after the worship set had ended. In the Old Testament, animals were sacrificed as an offering to God; however, it is continual offering from the heart that matters the most. God calls us to 'offer [our] bodies as a living sacrifice',[17] to lay down our lives daily before Him and trust Him to lead us in everything. It was His passion to walk this life with me every single day in every single moment and even though He knew my end from my beginning, it was His desire to have a conversation with me every day. It wasn't just about arriving at a destination at the end of life, it was allowing Jesus to daily walk with me on the journey.

After leaving university with a terrible debt against my name, I witnessed God restore my financial position. Before I had given my life to Jesus, I was very careless about the way I handled my finances. Spending on credit, not paying back money on time left my credit history in a huge mess. However, after Jesus had come into my life I would pray and ask Him to give me wisdom[18] over my finances. During that season I began to handle things in a way I hadn't known before. I believe God enabled me to view things from a different standpoint. Over a period of time my debts were cleared and my credit rating restored. The things I may have easily overlooked were the very things Jesus was concerned about.

I also earned an awful reputation at work for calling in sick on numerous occasions, sometimes because I was

---

[17] Romans 12:1.

[18] See James 1:5.

genuinely not feeling well, but there were also many times I just found an excuse not to go in. Again, I witnessed the power of restoration that came through placing my faith in Jesus. For a period of nearly two years I didn't need to call in sick once. Jesus was able to restore my well-being and reputation. It wasn't His will for me to live in debt and it wasn't His will that I should live unwell. Jesus made the ordinary moments in life become extraordinary. His kindness and caring heart desired to be part of all the small intricate details of my life that I may not have always seen as important.

As well as working my nine-to-five job, I was actively involved in church ministry during the week. Although it was amazing to be given the privilege to serve, and witness Jesus do amazing things, I was learning that friendship with God was what was more important. Jesus desired communion above everything else. He never switched Himself off and was always listening and ready to pour His love into my heart, wherever I was. He was after someone that would simply enjoy Him for Himself. In putting Jesus first, I found that everything around me fell into place.

As my heart was set towards Jesus, my thoughts were filled with a desire to please Him. The decisions I now made in life were centred on Him rather than me. I was beginning to see that God didn't just want to come and change areas of my life. He exchanged His life for mine; that which had been lost, He desired to fully restore. Spending time with Jesus gave me the eyes to see the worth of Him in all that was around me. Now that He lived in me, my entire outlook on life had changed.

It felt like everything was as it should be, until I came into the next phase of my journey, where I was about to learn some of the biggest lessons of my faith.

Chapter Six
Divided

Above all else, guard your heart, for everything
you do flows from it.
Proverbs 4:23

In the summer of 2010, I began a relationship with Noreen, who I am thankfully able to call my wife today, but back then things were not as straightforward as I hoped.

The funny thing is that a few years before my salvation took place, I actually tried to connect with Noreen through a social media platform. Her face came up on a mutual friend's list and at the time I thought, 'Well, she looks nice! I'd like to get to know her.' After sending her messages and hearing back from her, I found out she was someone who loved God. She seemed like a good Christian girl, but for me that was no-go territory, especially with my ungodly motives and lustful desires.

Things had changed after giving my life to Jesus. The way I now looked at women was different; I had a new respect for them and I would see them as daughters who were loved by a heavenly Father. One day while I was on social media, I reconnected with Noreen and shared with her what God was doing in my life, and not long after we eventually met for the first time at a Christian youth event. From that time on, we became good friends and we would often pray over the phone together and share testimonies of the things God was doing in our lives. Initially there was no intention to further our relationship. However, a year into our friendship I began to feel attracted to Noreen and also felt that God had shown me through a dream that we were meant to be together.

At this point I was extremely nervous. I had not been in a relationship since I had given my life to Jesus and it felt like an entirely new experience, even though I had previously been involved in relationships. I wasn't sure how I was meant to approach Noreen, but more than anything it was my desire to honour God and live in purity before Him. After spending much time in prayer and even getting advice from one of my pastors, I eventually decided to meet with Noreen to let her know about the way I felt.

Looking back at the day, it was a very strange and awkward scenario. I had somehow managed to pull myself together to share my heart with Noreen and asked her to meet me in Camden.

We walked around the area for a while before finding a random pub where we decided to sit down at a table outside. As we sat with our two pints of cola, our conversation was nothing out of the norm; however, in my head I was constantly trying to find the right moment and words to let Noreen know how I felt. I could tell she had no clue and that made me even more nervous because I had no idea as to what her response would be. I could feel my heart skipping a beat. Even though I was sat in conversation, my mind wasn't engaged – everything Noreen was saying was going over my head. It felt like I had been sitting there for an entire day before I had the courage to eventually tell her how I felt. Even though I could feel my face turning as red as a tomato, there was a huge relief on the inside when I finally told her. Noreen's response was unusually calm, given that it was all a bit unexpected. She told me she would pray into it, and for me that actually seemed like the best thing she could have said – I was just happy that she didn't reject me. On her way home, Noreen asked God to speak to her about our friendship and soon after she also began to feel that there was more to our relationship.

From then on, we entered into a season of courtship which we both felt would eventually lead us into marriage. Initially things were going really well. We both had several confirmations in which we felt God strongly speak to us about being together and I was convinced she was the one God had chosen for me. However, about a year after the beginning of our courtship, things became complicated between us. We would argue and disagree over small things and I began to think that the relationship was never from God to begin with.

My thoughts became centred around my relationship with Noreen rather than God and in all the commotion I lost my focus on Jesus. I should have been drawing near to Him, but instead I withdrew into my frustrations and allowed my heart to become hardened. It wasn't that I stopped loving Jesus, but I knew within myself that I had lost giving Him my undivided attention. I wasn't prioritising my time with Him; I was choosing to figure out for myself whether or not I could make the relationship work without living in continual submission to Jesus. When I stepped outside of walking in intimacy with God, my life was functioning through the carnal nature rather than being led by the Holy Spirit. Living carnally would satisfy my flesh, but it could never represent who Jesus was, let alone honour and please Him.

> So I say, live by the Spirit, and you will not gratify the desires of the flesh. For the flesh desires what is contrary to the Spirit, and the Spirit what is contrary to the flesh.
> *Galatians 5:16-17a*

The situation between Noreen and me was getting worse and our relationship was falling apart. We both decided to take some time out to fast and pray as we desperately needed Jesus to intervene and give us direction in how He wanted us to move forward. By the end of the fast, Noreen was sure that she had heard from God that the relationship was going to work and that we were meant to see things through. I, on the other hand, hadn't heard anything further from God; I was certain that He had nothing more to say and I couldn't see things working out between us. Without there being an agreement on both sides, I couldn't see us progressing any further and so our relationship finally came to an end. We went our separate ways, deciding that it would be best to no longer stay in touch. It was complete closure, to the point that I deleted Noreen's number and even removed her from my friends list on social media. I needed a fresh start, and this seemed the only way after all that had happened between us.

It was only after my break-up with Noreen that I realised how divided my heart had become. I had drifted away from my first love[19] and it felt like I had cheated on Jesus. Ultimately, it was my choice to make time for the things I treasured in life, but I had been so caught up in my relationship with Noreen that I had become distracted from the One who was supposed to mean everything to me. My love for Jesus was compromised and He no longer had first place. How I was living my 'Christian' life on the outside did not line up with what was in my heart. The moment I thought I had it all worked out in my head was the moment I became independent from the need of His presence. I was trying to achieve success in my relationship with Noreen outside of the presence of God, and that was only going to turn out to be lifeless.

I knew I had the choice to repent and lay my life down before Jesus. I could either come to Him in the nakedness of my sin or hide and cover myself up with the things of this world. I could pretend that everything was OK, but deep down there remained a void that only Jesus could fill. I was learning that being vulnerable in my relationship with God wasn't a weak thing; it was the very place where God could display His strength and glory. This is why it is so important to live a lifestyle dependent upon God; without Him, success has no definition. I also knew that Jesus wasn't looking for someone who was perfect, but

---

[19] See Revelation 2:4.

rather someone who understood the need for Him in order to live.

Things needed to get repositioned in my heart. Jesus wanted centre place. Although I had neglected Him, He had never closed the door to me. He wanted to be my first love again, and I was ready to give up everything so I could have all of Him.

Once things had calmed down after my split with Noreen, I had time to gather my emotions. It was during this time that I could hear the Holy Spirit tugging on my heart, simply saying, 'Come back to me.' Even though I messed up, never for a moment did He hold it against me. Jesus was always there waiting for me to return to Him and once I did, I realised how desperately I needed Him and how broken I was without Him.

Only when my heart was once again captivated by Jesus could I truly see how far I had let myself go from His presence. His light was able to illuminate every dark area of my life. The issue wasn't that I had taken my eyes off Him, it was the fact that I wasn't looking at Him for long enough. He was the source of life and true fulfilment, so lack of fellowship with Him meant lack of life. Living in union with Jesus never meant that everything would be perfect; it meant that I could still have Him and be satisfied, regardless of all the complications this life may bring. Only Jesus could truly give purpose in all of life's issues. God was reminding me that I could trust Him, even with the things that were close to my heart.

In every season, in simply turning my attention towards Jesus and giving Him my undivided time, I have learned that in the light of His presence all the lesser things in life fade away. 'In every Christian's heart there is a cross and a throne, and the Christian is on the throne till he puts himself on the cross. If he refuses the cross he remains on the throne.'[20] The throne is the place from which Jesus wants to rule as the King inside of our hearts. His love and rulership cannot be compromised. Until we surrender all, we will remain the rulers of our own lives. It is only in living a life of surrender that the true experience of our union with Jesus will be found. This is where we can live hearing the very heartbeat of God.

---

[20] A W Tozer, *The Radical Cross: Living the Passion of Christ* (Chicago, IL: Moody Publishers, 2015), p 138 (Kindle edition), location 1313-1314.

Chapter Seven
Encounter

John answered them all, 'I baptise you with water.
But one who is more powerful than I will come,
the straps of whose sandals I am not worthy to
untie. He will baptise you with the Holy Spirit
and fire.'
Luke 3:16

Learning from my past mistakes, I made a decision that I wasn't going to let anything stop me from pursuing Jesus above everything else. There wasn't anything wrong in me being in a relationship with Noreen; the issue was that my love for Jesus had been compromised. Once more, as my life was laid down at His feet and my heart surrendered, He began to fill me with a hunger for Himself. There came a deep cry on the inside of me, longing to know Him more. God was after someone who would seek Him with no other motive than to simply love Him. It was in this season of my life that I pursued Him, leaving no excuses to relentlessly go after Him with all that I had.

At the beginning of 2012, my cousin told me that a respected evangelist was going to be holding some revival meetings in the north-east of England. Nathan Morris was an evangelist who led a ministry called Shake The Nations. I was never someone who watched much Christian television, but I distinctly remembered watching evangelist Nathan preach at the 'Bay of the Holy Spirit'. This was a move of God that had taken place in Mobile, Alabama, in the United States, starting in 2010. Thousands gathered night after night to encounter God's presence and multitudes were touched and healed by Jesus. On several occasions while I was watching the broadcast at home, the presence of God became strong and flooded the room. It was so powerful and tangible that there were times I got down on my knees on the living room floor and worshipped Jesus.

You can imagine the excitement after my cousin first told me about the meetings. I got on the phone straight away to book my tickets and began to plan my journey well in advance. This was one of those meetings I wasn't going to miss! Although I hadn't attended anything like this before, I could feel a stirring of expectancy in my spirit. I was going in anticipation that I would have an encounter with Jesus.

The time had finally come. It was March. Some friends and I made a four-hour-long journey up to Hull in East Yorkshire to attend the revival meetings. Over the course of the next three days I witnessed things that I could only recall taking place in the Scriptures. From the moment we arrived at the meetings, countless lives were being touched by Jesus and filled with the Holy Spirit, and people were being healed, both physically and emotionally. I remember someone getting out of a wheelchair after being prayed for. I had never seen anything like it – the same Jesus who healed throughout the Scriptures was healing in those meetings, and you could sense the power of the Holy Spirit was very present. 'Jesus went throughout Galilee, teaching in their synagogues, proclaiming the good news of the kingdom, and healing every disease and illness among the people' (Matthew 4:23).

There were several occasions in which I also received prayer through the laying on of hands.[21] As I witnessed others step forward to receive prayer, there were many who would fall down as they were overcome by the power of the Holy Spirit. In the past I had witnessed others having similar encounters, but I had never experienced this for myself. However, after having hands laid on me when I went forward to receive prayer, it felt like an electric current went through my body and I fell to the ground as I wasn't able to stand. The manifest presence of God overwhelmed me as I experienced His power going through my body.

In the Old Testament we learn that in Solomon's day, the Ark of the Covenant was placed in the temple he had built. The ark was a wooden chest with gold laid over the top and was seen as symbolic of God's presence. When it was brought into the temple there was a cloud that filled the place and the priests could not continue ministering.[22] In the New Covenant, those who trust Jesus become God's

---

[21] See 1 Timothy 4:14. Spiritual gifts can be transferred by believers laying hands on one another.
[22] See 1 Kings 8:10-11.

ark; He comes and dwells in us. That same cloud, the presence of God, now lived in me. When I was overwhelmed by the presence of God, I had a physical reaction – sometimes we may experience a 'temporary, physical response to a spiritual encounter with God'.[23]

Throughout the meetings I was also given the privilege to hear some inspiring sermons from several other speakers who all delivered powerful messages. As each of them shared their hearts, there was something very special about their personal relationship with the Holy Spirit which I was drawn to. I knew that there was more that Jesus had for me, and as the days progressed, the hunger for Him increased.

We finally came to the last day. My friends and I felt extremely blessed in all that God had poured into our lives over the past few days. Jesus had met with each of us in a profound way; something fresh was deposited on the inside and I was going back home with His fire burning in my heart.

Our plan was to head back to London on the Saturday afternoon after we had attended an outreach taking place in the market square. There was still one more evening session that remained, but I hadn't made plans to attend as I wanted to get back in good time for my commitments at church the following day. It was nearly time for us to leave and head back home, but my friends were eager to stay for the final meeting. I was slightly frustrated as we had already planned to head home that afternoon. Still,

[23] David Diga Hernandez, *Carriers of the Glory: Becoming a Friend of the Holy Spirit* (Shippensburg, PA: Destiny Image Publishers, 2016), p 177 (Kindle edition), location 3134.

my friends were persistent, and to make things worse there were other believers in the market square who were encouraging us to make sure not to miss it!

I couldn't remember the last time I had missed a Sunday service at church. I was fully committed to serving every week and I took my responsibilities very seriously, but in that instant I felt God soften my heart. If Jesus had something more for us, why should I be the one to get in the way? Although I was open to the possibility of attending the final meeting, I already knew it was fully booked, so there wasn't much hope. Despite that, I gave my friends the opportunity to see if they could find a way for us to be there. Lo and behold, within a matter of minutes they had somehow managed to find some spare tickets that someone was giving away! I could not believe what was happening. I wasn't used to these spontaneous moments, but I ended up making the relevant phone calls to let everyone know that I would be arriving back home later than expected so that we could attend the final meeting.

Before the meeting began, we decided to take a short nap in the car as we were all feeling exhausted. I wasn't sure what to expect that night but, as always, I kept my heart open to Jesus. I knew there was always more for me in His presence. Once it was nearly time, we made our way to the venue. Three of the four tickets we had were for seats in the balcony and the other one was for a single seat on the ground floor. I suggested that I would take the single seat and let my friends sit together; there was a part of me that wanted to take this seat because it was closer to the front, and it also gave me some space to have some time alone.

Once I had taken my seat I got talking to a gentleman named Ted who was sitting next to me. He seemed a kind man, and we shared a little about our lives before the meeting began. We were both excited about what God had in store for us that evening.

From the moment worship began I could sense the atmosphere being distinctly different from what I had experienced over the past few days. There was so much hunger and expectation in the room that I could feel it on my skin. As the evening went on, the manifest presence of God thickened and it was as if a blanket of His glory covered the auditorium. I had been present in many services in the past where I had sensed the presence of God, but this was on another level. The only way I can describe it is that I could tangibly feel the weight of God's glory and it felt as if rain from heaven was pouring down.

It became so intense that the worship team couldn't even stand any longer. I remember hearing others around me who were wailing and crying out to God. It also sounded like there were many who were being freed from demonic bondage right where they were sitting.[24] It felt like Jesus had walked into the room; there was so much freedom that the entire place had come into an encounter with Him. 'Where the Spirit of the Lord is, there is freedom' (2 Corinthians 3:17).

The glory of God filled the room; it felt as if Jesus was so near that if I had reached out, I would have been able to touch Him. It came to a point that I became so unaware

---

[24] See Acts 8:7. During Jesus' ministry on earth, He cast out demons, and that same authority is given to believers – see Matthew 10:1; Mark 16:17.

of myself and surroundings that even with hundreds of people around me, it was just me and Jesus. I could feel Him come and rest upon my heart. I became so awestruck and overwhelmed by His presence that I was left speechless, with only tears remaining. In every heartbeat I could feel Jesus giving Himself to me in a deeper way, and this was leaving me completely undone. He was so present that the Holy Spirit even convicted me for taking the seat which I selfishly chose for myself. As silly as it may sound, it broke my heart that I could hurt Him in such a way.

The encounter only intensified throughout the evening. My legs began to feel like jelly and I began to physically feel heat go through my body. Eventually I wasn't able to stand, so I sat back down. Ted placed his arm around me to let me know that he was there. In that moment it suddenly felt as if a volcano had erupted over me; it felt like my body had been set on fire. I was so hot that I perspired to the extent that my clothes were soaked through. I had never experienced anything like this before and yet it was something I did not want to end as I encountered His presence.

In the book of Corinthians Paul speaks of such encounters, in which he did not know whether he was 'in the body or out of the body'.[25] This is one way to illustrate what I was going through. It felt like I had entered into another realm. For the very first time I began to see open-eyed visions and throughout the evening, while I was praying in tongues, I started to understand some of the words that were completely unknown to my natural

---

[25] 2 Corinthians 12:2.

mind.[26] The entire experience felt like an endless river flowing from within me. It was one of the most beautiful and profound encounters with Jesus I've ever had.

At the end of the night I was reunited with my friends. It was amazing to see how God had also touched them in different ways. As we were preparing to leave, Ted said to me that I should pray and ask God to lead me to a mentor who was 'Spirit-filled, birthed in the Word'. It was a little random at the time, so I didn't really think about it, and on top of that I was a complete wreck! I was so intoxicated by the Holy Spirit and filled with joy that my friends had to help me walk back to the car. Being filled with the Holy Spirit felt a bit like being drunk to me; it was, of course, in no way harmful to my body and it was definitely a happier and more fulfilling experience! When the initial infilling of the Holy Spirit took place on the day of Pentecost, Jesus' followers were seen to be as if they had been drinking.[27]

Following this encounter, my heart began to burn with a deep infatuation for Jesus and there was nothing in my life that meant more to me than wanting to be with Him. I may have never experienced these encounters had I been tied up in my previous relationship with Noreen. It wasn't that I went looking for an experience for the sake of an experience; rather, in my pursuit of Jesus, He gave me an experience of Himself. My life was marked by Him forever. The love of Jesus had left me in a complete wreck,

---

[26] The spiritual gift of 'interpretation' (1 Corinthians 12:10) is given by the Holy Spirit to supernaturally reveal messages spoken in an unknown tongue for the edifying of the Church.
[27] See Acts 2:15.

and I was hungrier for His presence than I had ever been before.

Chapter Eight
Visions

In the last days, God says, I will pour out my
Spirit on all people. Your sons and daughters will
prophesy, your young men will see visions, your
old men will dream dreams.
Acts 2:17

When I was in Hull, there were several things that Jesus revealed to me throughout my encounter. These experiences were not just life-changing, but they also enabled me to see the passion and desire that God burns with for His Church. The Holy Spirit took me on a journey into some of the depths and longings inside His heart. During this time, I had several visions and experiences.

In one of the visions, I had seen a place that looked as if it was the throne room of heaven. It was a huge auditorium-type setting; however, I could not see there being any walls or ceiling. In this place I sensed the entire atmosphere was saturated with the glory of God. In the midst of it all there was a magnificent light that illuminated everything. The source of the light was the One who was sitting on the throne, which was high above everything else. Though I could not see through this incredible light, I knew in my spirit that the One who was sat on the throne was Jesus and before Him was splendour and majesty. Below Him I saw a multitude who were gathered together in one accord; they were the bride of Jesus. They were all in awe, worshipping Him as they fixated themselves, looking at Him. As they were beholding Jesus, the light coming forth from Him was reflecting back over them and it was this light that made His bride shine with astounding beauty and purity, without spot and without blemish.[28] I could see that Jesus desired a bride that was so in love with Him that she wouldn't take her eyes off Him; a bride whose love was not compromised, a bride that was pure and holy.

I was overcome, firstly because it was the first time I had open-eyed visions, but primarily because I was in awe of what I was seeing before me. I always knew God was holy, but never had I felt such holiness as I did when I saw His bride worshipping Him. I could sense the Spirit of the fear of the Lord[29] was upon the bride as the people revered Jesus, in submission to Him. In that same instant my own heart became overwhelmed by God's holiness. Although Jesus was my friend and Bridegroom, He was the King of glory who had been set apart as the prize of all eternity. The revelation of His holiness pierced my being and left me undone. In all of this I am reminded of what John had

---

[28] See Ephesians 5:27.

[29] See Isaiah 11:2. This is the Spirit of the fear of the Lord, as in, being awestruck by Him.

seen in the book of Revelation when he saw Jesus, the Lamb upon the throne, being exalted and praised:

> Then I looked and heard the voice of many angels, numbering thousands upon thousands, and ten thousand times ten thousand. They encircled the throne and the living creatures and the elders. In a loud voice they were saying: 'Worthy is the Lamb, who was slain, to receive power and wealth and wisdom and strength and honour and glory and praise!'
> *Revelation 5:11-12*

During the second experience, Jesus took me into yet another profound encounter. This time it wasn't through a vision, but it was felt by my spirit. The best way I can describe it is that God had taken me on a journey into His heart. As I was drawn in, I first began to feel a deep cry of pain and anguish. It was the heartbeat of God crying out for humankind, for the hearts that He so deeply loved and desired to be with. After feeling this deep sadness in His heart, I then started to experience a sense of His overwhelming joy.

As I felt this joy, there came an impression in which I could feel God wanting to take each of us by the hand and dance with us as He rejoiced. He was so joyous over the way He had created us, and it made Him extremely happy. We meant so much more to Him than we could ever imagine. I do not have the words to describe the love I felt He had for humanity: it was far above what I could comprehend. During this experience I was taken back and forth from this joy into the deep cry inside of the heart of

Jesus. It was the most unexplainable feeling and yet it was more real to me than the air around me.

In the next instant, I began to feel a grieving in His heart. He was hurting because He desired to possess His Church with the Holy Spirit, but there were many who were not willing to surrender to His ways. Although the Holy Spirit was present in many churches, there was no manifestation of His person, because He hadn't been welcomed as the head of His bride.[30] It was always God's passion for His Church to experience the fullness of the Holy Spirit, but due to the lack of surrender to His rule, programmes were prioritised over His presence and power and this ultimately restricted the people's experience with Him. Jesus was deeply hurt; not only was He grieved by them, He was also grieving for them. There was so much more that God desired to do through the Holy Spirit; it was unimaginable to think what He could have done if there was total surrender. I once read a quote by Nathan Morris where he said, 'The Holy Spirit must be front and center in our meetings, because it is the Holy Spirit who reveals Jesus to the world.'[31] The presence of God is not just a theory and doctrine, Jesus is our 'ever-present help',[32] He is the very means by which we can now live. Without the Holy Spirit at the centre of all things, we may end up building something that was never intended

---

[30] See Colossians 1:18.

[31] Nathan Morris: Facebook post,

https://www.facebook.com/EvangelistNathan/photos/a.261699
983840103/1707061452637275/?type=3&theater (accessed 3rd
August 2019).

[32] Psalm 46:1.

by God. Without His presence there is room for 'dead religion' to keep us occupied with loveless duties and where the Holy Spirit is not present, anything we do is not of any true worth.

These extraordinary experiences had left me feeling overwhelmed and in awe of God's presence. More than seeing visions for the first time, it amazed me once again to perceive how real God truly was. He is still able to communicate to us in this present day. Jesus is a living person, someone with real emotions and real feelings. My own heart was torn into a million pieces as I felt His unfailing love towards us. Never had I felt such a longing in which I sensed God Himself weep for His own creation and at the same time feel His joy celebrating over us.

Lastly, it was during the same encounter that I first heard God calling me into the ministry. It wasn't an audible voice, but I could sense in my spirit there was a commissioning that took place. This was followed by several other visions which were all tied into my destiny, and over the years since, God has continued to confirm this through His speaking in various different ways. At the time I wasn't able to grasp all that God was doing, but I knew that He had planted a seed, and in due season He would cause those things to be brought to birth.

There was so much that God was doing in those few hours that even today I am still feeling the aftermath of what took place during my time in Hull. The revelations that I received then are still being processed through my life today and are drawing me closer to God's heart. I am just beginning to scratch the surface of the things that God has called me into. I want to encourage those of you who feel the calling of God over your lives. Some of you may have experienced a delay in seeing the things which you believe God has spoken to you come to fruition. God's timing is flawless. Live for His person and not for His promise. That which He has spoken will surely come to pass!

> Being confident of this, that he who began a good work in you will carry it on to completion until the day of Christ Jesus.
> *Philippians 1:6*

One of the things I have learned is that nothing will ever count unless its origin is found in the heart of the Father and unless it comes forth by the Holy Spirit. Many could have told me what I was called to do, but when I heard Jesus speak into my being, it changed everything. It went from me fulfilling my calling, to God now fulfilling His call through me. It's important to remember that God is the One who calls us, and not we ourselves. If it doesn't come from the Holy Spirit then we will always strive in our own strength. '"Not by might nor by power, but by my Spirit," says the LORD Almighty' (Zechariah 4:6). The Holy Spirit can do more in a moment where we are completely yielded than we can by being stuck in 'dead religion' for an entire lifetime.

Jesus had done a deep work through the Holy Spirit which marked my life forever. However, these life-changing experiences were not an end in themselves. There was no doubt that what had taken place in Hull was a landmark moment in my journey of faith. It was a moment when God deeply touched me, but it wasn't going to end there. Jesus had so much more in store for me than I could ever imagine.

> The reason He gives a public touch, is to draw
> you to a private kiss.
> *Eric Gilmour*[33]

---

[33] Eric Gilmour, *Honey: Drops of Sweet Life from the Mouth of the King* (Warsaw, IN: Tall Pine Books, 2019), p 52.

Chapter Nine
Inebriated

These people are not drunk, as you suppose. It's
only nine in the morning!
Acts 2:15

The adventure that started in Hull was far from over. Somehow, we managed to travel back to London straight after the meeting ended. It was a fairly long drive and by the time we arrived home it was the early hours of the morning. One of my friends decided to stay over with me. We were so exhausted that we went straight to bed and managed to get a few hours' sleep.

It wasn't long before I was awake again and although I hadn't slept much, I was surprisingly full of energy. From the moment I was up, there was a hunger in my heart to read the Scriptures. My family were away for the weekend and my friend was still sleeping, so the house was quiet. I took hold of my Bible and made my way to my mum's room so that I could have some alone time with Jesus. I got down on my knees, opened my Bible and began to read a scripture that the Holy Spirit had placed on my heart from the book of 2 Thessalonians: 'With this in mind, we constantly pray for you, that our God may make you worthy of his calling, and that by his power he may bring to fruition your every desire for goodness and your every deed prompted by faith' (2 Thessalonians 1:11).

As soon as I read this verse, I suddenly felt something burst on the inside of me and I began to pray in tongues. Once more, just like the previous night, His presence filled the atmosphere. I could feel my body getting hot again and the fire of the Holy Spirit burning in my heart. I knew that Jesus was already with me, but when I encountered Him during this moment, I could tangibly feel His manifest presence and sense His nearness.

Had I wanted to, I could have chosen not to yield to God, and let the moment pass. But if God had chosen to show up in such a way, I was more than ready to embrace Him. Although I couldn't fully comprehend all that Jesus was doing, I would rather have remained God-conscious and had an encounter with Him than become self-conscious and missed being touched by Him. Colossians 3:1-2 reminds us that it is important that we set our hearts on the things above, where Christ is seated, and not on earthly things.

My family returned home later that day while I was still caught up in God's presence. They could see I was having some sort of an encounter with the Holy Spirit. They had never seen me like this before and it seemed like they were a bit taken aback by everything. I was unrecognisable to myself, so I'm fairly sure it was an overwhelming experience for them as much as it was for me. However, they did let me pray with them and that was a precious time for us to experience God together. They were receptive to what the Holy Spirit was doing in the moment and, ever since, have been an incredible support in my journey of faith with Jesus.

Over the next few days the manifest presence of God which I experienced in Hull was just as present at home; it never left me. All I wanted to do was be alone with Jesus and stay lost in His presence. I was so overcome that I had to take some time off work so that I could spend time with Him. If Jesus wanted more for me, I wasn't going to get in the way. Throughout these days I was either weeping before Him or I was walking the streets praying in the Holy Spirit. His love swept me away, my heart was flooded with His reality and I was completely wrecked. One of the things that stuck with me from my time in Hull were the words that Ted spoke to me before we left, so I made it a point to take them before Jesus myself: 'God, lead me to a mentor who is Spirit-filled, birthed in the Word.'

Around two days after getting back, I was walking the streets near where I lived. I was still feeling inebriated from His presence and was enjoying every moment of being with Jesus. I remember it being a sunny day and I was heading towards the park so I could spend some time meditating on the things that God had done.

As I was turning the corner at the end of my road, I came across a building which I could not remember seeing before. I had lived in the area for many years, so it was fascinating to think about why I could not recall ever seeing it. One of the things that stood out to me was the words 'New Life'[34] written across the top of the building. I was instantly reminded of the church that had just hosted the revival meetings in Hull: they were also called New Life.[35] Nevertheless, I brushed it off, thinking it was an interesting coincidence and carried on with my journey. However, as I got to the gates of the park, I heard the Holy Spirit clearly telling me to turn around and go back.

Once I walked back and stood at the entrance of the building, I realised it was actually a small church. I was intrigued and curious to find out more about what to me was an unusual-looking place – a small building with trees around it, not really my idea of a church – so I stepped forward onto the lawn. Suddenly I could sense the tangible weight of God's presence; it felt like I had stepped onto holy ground, something that had been consecrated to God. I sensed that this was a place that was saturated with prayers – I could just feel it in my spirit. Before I knew it, a man got out of a car which was parked beside the building and stood next to me. As crazy as it might sound, without any introduction we both began to pray aloud in the Holy Spirit. It was so out of this world: I had never met this man before and yet for some reason, it never for a moment made me feel awkward. Eventually, after praying, we briefly introduced ourselves and it turned out that the man was actually the pastor of the church. After finding out when they gathered to meet, I simply carried on about my day.

Over the next few days I couldn't help but remember what Ted had encouraged me to pray about, that God

<hr />

[34] New Life Christian Centre, Edgware.

[35] Now called Revive Church.

would lead me to a mentor who was 'Spirit-filled, birthed in the Word'. The Holy Spirit had led me to this unknown church to meet a pastor that I had not known before. In that way, God had literally answered that very prayer.

I was certain that God was speaking to me about transitioning from the church which I was currently serving, but it took a while for me to get my head around it. In the following weeks, I began to ask God for clarity and direction, as I needed to be sure that I was hearing Him clearly. As well as being involved within leadership, I had also developed many healthy relationships with my church family. It never made complete sense as to why God wanted me to leave, but I could not ignore the fact that the Holy Spirit was convicting my heart to do so. God was leading me into a new phase and therefore wanted to plant me elsewhere; it was no coincidence that I had met the pastor of the New Life Church. God prepared my heart to move on. This is where Jesus wanted me to be for the next season of my journey with Him. However, the transition wasn't going to be as smooth as I thought it would be.

Being obedient to God wasn't always going to be comfortable and straightforward. After deciding it was time to transition, I consulted my leadership at church, but not everyone was in agreement with my choices.

It was time to move on and that wasn't easy for everyone to grasp, including myself. Regardless of which church I attended, it was always my desire to maintain my relationships, but sadly many of my close friendships within the church dissolved. It was a painful and trying time, but living in obedience to Jesus was what truly mattered. In saying 'yes' to Him, I found fulfilment in my heart.

> Obedience is not measured by our ability to obey laws and principles, obedience is measured by our response to God's voice.
> *Bill Johnson*[36]

In the next chapter of my journey, my experience of church was very different from what I had previously experienced. In my conversations with some of my friends it was referred to as the 'secret church'. The building itself was much smaller in size, and the numbers in the congregation reflected that. I was used to flashy lights and big screens, and this church didn't have such. But the most important thing was that Jesus was very present and I deeply encountered His presence.

Every time we met together at New Life, I could never predict what was going to happen during the services. Sometimes we would just sit and wait in God's presence for hours, and at other times it would feel like heaven joined us during worship. It was all centred around God's presence and letting the Holy Spirit lead the service. This was something that I had not come across before. Naturally speaking, it seemed like everything was stripped down, but spiritually there was a weight of God's presence and so much freedom to encounter Jesus. When

---

[36] Bill Johnson, cited in Kris Vallotton's Twitter Feed, https://twitter.com/kvministries/status/616592381283057664?s= 20 (accessed 3rd August 2019).

everything that I was used to was taken away, I realised how dependent I needed to become upon God's presence.

God also began to build a healthy relationship between me and the pastor. God really used him during this season to be an encouragement in my life. He was someone that genuinely wanted me to grow in my walk with Jesus. This senior leader became a good friend and a father-type figure to me. It was always his heart's passion to see the body of Christ equipped and sent out. I'd often hear him say that he was doing his job well when the church was empty, as that meant we were out there doing what God had called us to do.

After my encounter in Hull, something drastically shifted in my heart and it gave me a burning desire for Jesus that put Him above everything else. I had witnessed first-hand how God was supernaturally able to align my relationships and place me exactly where I needed to be for the season I was going through. I was learning how important it is to know that God's heart is to see His family extend beyond the four walls of a building. It was more important to live in obedience to Jesus than to seek the approval of others and what they may think is best. This was all so powerful to experience, and it became a precious season in my life in which my addiction to God's presence grew. I had nothing else to live for other than Him and I found my new favourite place in the entire world was to sit at the feet of Jesus.

Chapter Ten
Intimacy

*One thing I ask from the LORD, this only do I
seek: that I may dwell in the house of the LORD all
the days of my life, to gaze on the beauty of the
LORD and to seek him in his temple.*
Psalm 27:4

In the time I have walked with Jesus, I have been so
privileged to witness and encounter things that I could
only have dreamed were possible. If there is one thing I
have learned, it is that the presence of God is the treasure
of all life.

It is like the man we hear about in Matthew 13:44 who
found treasure 'hidden in a field … hid it again, and then
in his joy went and sold all he had and bought that field'.
There is no possible way to place a value on God's
presence, but even if we sold all that we had to take
possession of it, it is a joyful sacrifice in which we do not
lose anything. The fact that He has given Himself to us

should be enough for us to love Him above everything else.

The only way our journey with Jesus will ever be sustained is through continual intimate fellowship with Him. Unless the foundation of His presence is laid, without intimacy in our walk with Jesus, we merely disguise ourselves with a form of religion. Where there is lack of communion with Him, ultimately there will always be a lack of contentment in life itself. Jesus satisfies us to the degree that we have given our hearts to Him; only when He becomes everything can we live satisfied by Him.

In the Psalms we hear some of the most valuable words that can help us understand how to live a life of intimacy sustained by Jesus: 'I keep my eyes always on the LORD' (Psalm 16:8). David, the shepherd boy who became the king of Israel, is the author of this beautiful psalm, and although he made mistakes, it seems he was a man who kept his eyes on the Lord. No matter what we may go through in life, God is more real than what we see around us, and I believe we are given the ability to see Him in every circumstance. If we choose to look at Him long enough, we will see that the beauty that emanates from His face is more captivating than anything this world could ever give to us. To cultivate our love and intimacy with Jesus, we must continually set Jesus before our hearts and intentionally pursue Him in our desire to be with Him.

It is easy to display intimacy in a public setting when we worship God on a Sunday morning; however, God desires our hearts in the private place and it is here that we develop a lifestyle of worship before God. When the disciples asked Jesus how to pray, He told them to go into their own rooms, shut the door and pray in secret where no one could see.[37] Intimacy with God is not defined by the latest worship song we can listen to, it is defined by getting alone and being with Him. This is the highest calling we can ever receive in life, one where Jesus calls us to Himself. This is the greatest invitation the world has ever been given.

> The highest priority in life is to intimately know Jesus.
> *Brian Guerin*[38]

Only in private are we able to experience Jesus in a way that we could not otherwise know Him. It is behind closed doors through intimacy that married couples are able to conceive a child. Here we find a sacred love that unites them as one flesh. It is in private that we find a place reserved for lovers; it is here that husband and wife share between them intimate moments which are not displayed for the world to see. We too, when we are alone with God, can experience a divine love exchange; we can conceive the very desires in His heart, and it is through intimacy that God births vision in us. In this place, God unveils His deep love to us through His Spirit, and is able to transform us to look like Him. It is in this union of intimacy that we can truly experience the oneness that God calls us to.

---

[37] See Matthew 6:6.

[38] https://youtu.be/tV1X6I-n1u8 (accessed 3rd August 2019).

> Nobody gets pregnant holding hands. Getting intimate with Jesus is the only way to be fruitful.
> *Eric Gilmour*[39]

Our relationship with Jesus won't steward itself. It's not merely about seeing how He can fit into our routines, but rather how we can prioritise our time and centre our lives around Him. Some may see this as religious works, but the truth is that we all make time for the things we value most in life, so how much more should it be with Jesus? No relationship can reach its full potential unless time is consistently invested. In valuing His presence, we recognise the worth of His love and at the same time see the need to live in dependency before Him. Without His presence in our lives we simply cannot fully live; living in complete abandonment is the perfect place to experience His manifest presence.

Intimacy with God is not some type of movement, or an optional extra for some believers. Everything God wishes to accomplish through our lives needs to come through an overflow of our relationship with Him. Some might say that we shouldn't live by our experiences. I completely agree – I think it is unbiblical to chase after an experience for the sake of an experience. It is also true that sometimes our feelings can mislead us. However, when we set our gaze towards Jesus and seek intimacy with Him, when we allow Him to captivate our hearts, Jesus Himself becomes our experience. We must also remember that our stories are all unique, as are our personalities and

---

[39] Eric Gilmour, *Union: The Thirsting Soul Satisfied in God* (Warsaw, IN: Tall Pine Books, 2018), p 129.

characters. God chooses to reveal Himself to us in different ways, but at the same time He remains the source of any truly meaningful spiritual experience.

> He whispers to some and shakes others. To some He speaks through an ocean and to others through the beauty of a desert sunrise.
> *Michael Koulianos*[40]

Throughout my journey, I have been able to see countless lives touched and transformed by Jesus. I've had the privilege to minister and serve God in different capacities during different seasons of my life. However, I have been deeply convicted when a love has developed for ministry more than my love for God Himself. After ministering, on several occasions, the Holy Spirit began to work deeply in the motives of my heart. God needed to sever pride from beneath me, and when He did, I would lay on my face before Him and realise the pulpit can never replace a love for His presence. He desired purity over pride. Jesus reminded me that He was enough and able to satisfy more than anything else. If I didn't see one more miracle, the fact that I had Jesus was the greatest miracle and it made every moment of life worth living.

We should never take our communion with God for granted and think we can do life without Him. In forfeiting the daily need of His presence, we lack the integrity to carry the message of reconciliation.[41] Unless

---

[40] Michael Koulianos, *Holy Spirit: The One Who Makes Jesus Real* (Shippensburg, PA: Destiny Image Publishers, 2017), p 43.
[41] See 2 Corinthians 5:18.

we stay in continual fellowship with Him, our hearts can become callous and insensitive. Although fruit may be seen on the outside, it is more important that God develops fruit in our own hearts – the fruit we read about in Galatians 5:22-23: 'But the fruit of the Spirit is love, joy, peace, forbearance, kindness, goodness, faithfulness, gentleness and self-control.' Godly character and substance are only truly produced in one's heart when we learn to yield to the Holy Spirit and allow Him to transform us into the image of Jesus.

> As Jesus and his disciples were on their way, he came to a village where a woman named Martha opened her home to him. She had a sister called Mary, who sat at the Lord's feet listening to what he said. But Martha was distracted by all the preparations that had to be made. She came to him and asked, 'Lord, don't you care that my sister has left me to do the work by myself? Tell her to help me!'
>
> 'Martha, Martha,' the Lord answered, 'you are worried and upset about many things, but few things are needed – or indeed only one. Mary has chosen what is better, and it will not be taken away from her.'
> *Luke 10:38-42*

In the scripture above we see a contrast – the sisters are two very different people – Martha, the one who was distracted by her efforts of hospitality, preparing a meal to feed Jesus and His disciples; Mary, on the other hand, sitting at Jesus' feet, in fellowship with Him, being 'fed' by Jesus. We hear at the end that Jesus commends Mary for her actions and says that she has chosen what is better. When we look to Jesus, He will empower us to become that which He has spoken to us.

Jesus does not look for factory workers to complete things on His behalf. He desires intimate lovers that seek true friendship with Him, with whom He can partner to bring His will to the earth. Just before Jesus died on the cross, He said the three most powerful words humanity would ever hear: 'It is finished' (John 19:30). There is nothing we can add through our works to what Jesus has already completed through His death. When He died, He took the punishment for our sin, the separation from God that we deserve. This is all a free gift, God's 'grace'; we cannot work to earn it. This is the New Covenant. As Ephesians 2:8-9 tells us: 'For it is by grace you have been saved, through faith – and this is not from yourselves, it is the gift of God – not by works, so that no one can boast.'

There were numerous ways in which God could have chosen to accomplish His will on earth, but He chose to do so by making His home in us. This shows how deeply God desires to be close to us. The New Covenant enables us to have direct contact with Him; it enables us to cease from a place of striving and enter into a place of rest that only Jesus can give to us. In giving us the Holy Spirit, He gave us all the ability to intimately walk with Him; through His manifest presence we can sense and perceive all that He is. God invites us all to come and sit with Him so that He, the 'bread of life',[42] can feed us with food that will satisfy every part of us.

---

[42] John 6:35.

Jesus is the true source of life and only He is the reward that brings fulfilment to our being. Although He gives His promises, let us never forsake His person. Nowhere else do we find a love that is perfect and complete other than in the person of Jesus. He is gentle, kind and more attractive than anything we can ever imagine. In His presence we discover the fullness of joy, peace and pleasure that is nowhere else to be found. It is the longing of the Bridegroom, Jesus Himself, that we be drawn in by His love, and become a bride that will love Him wholeheartedly.[43] He desires intimate friendship that will only be found in fellowship and this is why intimacy with God must always remain as our highest priority. It is here we find all the worth of life.

---

[43] See Matthew 22:37.

Chapter Eleven
Restored

*For you know that it was not with perishable
things such as silver or gold that you were
redeemed from the empty way of life handed down
to you from your ancestors, but with the precious
blood of Christ, a lamb without blemish or defect.*
1 Peter 1:18-19

The plan for redemption was written in God's heart long before He had created the world. In the book of Revelation, Jesus is seen as 'the Lamb who was slain from the creation of the world' (Revelation 13:8), meaning that before the world was created, God had already purposed for His beloved Son to be the perfect sacrifice for the sins of humanity. It was always part of His perfect plan to bring restoration to our lives. Not only was the blood of Jesus able to restore our fellowship with Him, but when we place our faith in Jesus, God adopts us into His own family. We go from once living as slaves to sin, to receiving the Spirit of sonship.[44] As God's children we become heirs of His promises and by His grace we have been given the privilege to share in the inheritance of Jesus.[45]

Over the years I can bear witness to the love of our heavenly Father. From the time I first gave my life to Jesus, up until now, I have seen the redemptive power of the cross continually working in and through my life. When things have been going well and through seasons where I faced trials and challenges, God has remained faithful. He has always kept His promises, and as a good Father it's His desire to bless me and fulfil all that He has spoken through His Word.

> Being confident of this, that he who began a good work in you will carry it on to completion until the day of Christ Jesus.
> *Philippians 1:6*

Nine months had now passed since my relationship with Noreen ended and we hadn't been in touch since. In October of that same year (2012) there was a two-day youth event taking place, which I was invited to go to, but I did not initially make plans to attend. However, I managed to win an all-expenses-paid ticket. I saw this as a sign that God wanted me to go. Little did I know that Noreen was going to be present at this very event.

On the second night, a group of friends and I were going to join together in a time of prayer. Just before we

---

[44] See Romans 8:15.

[45] See Galatians 3:29; Romans 8:17.

made our way to the prayer room, I went to ask a friend if they wanted to join us. Noreen was sitting close by and I thought it would be rude of me not to ask her to come along. This could have potentially been an awkward moment for me, but it wasn't. Out of courtesy and with no strings attached, I casually invited her to join us, and she agreed.

Somehow, by the end of the night, Noreen and I ended up praying for each other and by the end of the event itself, God had restored our friendship. It did cross my mind that maybe Noreen was actually the one for me, but I wasn't sure if it was just my flesh reacting or something genuine in my heart. I had come so far in my walk with Jesus that I was scared to make the same mistakes that I did before. Instead of being hasty and approaching Noreen, I decided that I would take it before Jesus and let Him speak to me.

After several months of praying and fasting, I was given a 'green light' by the Holy Spirit to talk to Noreen and let her know how I felt. I believe that God gave me a desire for Noreen and whether or not she felt the same way, I was ready to speak to her about it. We eventually arranged a time to meet together and I shared my heart with her about the way I felt. This was different from the first time. I felt a supernatural confidence in what God had spoken and nothing could persuade me otherwise.

Even though I was so sure this was God, I was a bit of a nervous wreck when it came to actually telling her. I remember having butterflies in my stomach that day in March 2013, with no idea as to what her response would be. Thankfully, it was a positive outcome. Noreen felt the same and God had also confirmed to her that we were meant to be together. That was a day I'll never forget. I

103

was filled with so much joy and excitement. There was no hesitation as to whether things were going to work out – we both knew that this was always meant to be.

Within a few weeks we had both told our families, and they were extremely happy for us. Initially we planned to get married the following year. However, God spoke to us and began to tell us about His plans. I heard the Holy Spirit specifically telling me that we were to get married in November that same year. Logically it didn't make sense; at the time I heard the Lord, we were already in the month of July and had just become officially engaged. We weren't prepared financially or mentally. I don't think we could grasp how close November was, being just a few months off. However, I couldn't steer away from God's voice; if He said it, I knew He would somehow do it.

Over the course of the next few weeks some of our close friends began to pray and prophesy[46] over us. Not one, but several of them had prophesied that they saw us getting married in November. That was really helpful as I'm pretty sure both our families thought I was crazy at one point!

It wasn't an easy journey, but we had to remain faithful in obedience to Jesus and give our 'yes' to Him. Everything came together and just seven months after we had told our parents, Noreen walked up the aisle in her beautiful white dress and became my wife. That was by far the happiest day of my life after giving my life to Jesus, and what a wonderful testimony it was to the promises of God.

---

[46] See 1 Corinthians 14:1. Prophecy is a gift of the Spirit where a person can discern and share a message from God.

When we prioritise Jesus and give Him first place in our hearts, we will realise that He is more than anything we could have asked for to begin with. During the period in which Noreen and I went our separate ways, the Holy Spirit worked a deep surgery in my heart. There was an alignment that needed to take place in which Jesus had to become everything to me. My desires were stripped back till Jesus was the only desire, and it was at this point that everything else in my life could fall into place.

> But seek first his kingdom and his righteousness,
> and all these things will be given to you as well.
> *Matthew 6:33*

If it's not all Jesus that we are seeking to glorify; there can be a mixture of motives within us and our hearts become impure. Although it was always my desire to one day get married, I needed to put God above my desire and give Him first place. When we truly seek Him with all of our heart, all the things in life, including the things that are important to us, will align to the will of God at the right time.

I can testify to God's faithfulness. He has always kept His word. Later on, my wife gave birth to our first child and together we are able to enjoy the life which God promises to us in the New Covenant, a life that trusts and leans upon God and recognises that Jesus is enough.

While working my nine-to-five job, at the end of 2017 the Holy Spirit led Noreen and I to officially launch our ministry, Kingdom Encounter. Today it is with great joy that as a family we are witnessing many come into a living encounter with Jesus. Our hearts' desire is to build a platform for the presence and glory of God and our mission is to see lives encounter Jesus and be transformed by the power of the Holy Spirit. Throughout the year we host conferences, outreaches and encounter meetings. We've been privileged to work alongside churches across the UK and see God's people equipped and empowered by His presence. Over the past few years we have witnessed the sick healed, the oppressed set free and countless hearts given to Jesus. We believe God has called us into regions and local communities to raise up disciples of Jesus who will love and live radically for Him. As we continue to proclaim the good news of Jesus, we are believing that we will see a harvest of Jesus-lovers raised up and equipped to walk in the fullness of the Holy Spirit. This is the heartbeat of heaven, that humanity would come into a living experience of Jesus; to know Him intimately is where all of life's purposes will be found.

I am forever grateful to Jesus, who, in His mercy, chose to love me and lay down His life for mine. My life held no true purpose and value until one day the Holy Spirit led me to the One who was Jesus. He was more real than anything I had ever known, a real person, and only He was able to transform my heart and rewrite my story. He is that same Jesus today, and the Holy Spirit is the One who continues to lead me.

I cannot dare to imagine what my life would have looked like without Him, for without Him there is no life at all. I have experienced His faithfulness and goodness throughout every season. Everything I've ever needed has always been found in God's presence, and it is His presence that satisfies above all things. May we always remember God's gift to humanity, the sacrifice of His own

Son, Jesus. By His blood we have been cleansed and made new. This is my story of going from death to life, where Jesus came and rescued me from 'darkness into his wonderful light' (1 Peter 2:9).

Chapter Twelve
Come!

Come to me, all you who are weary and burdened,
and I will give you rest.
Matthew 11:28

I wanted to end this book by extending an invitation. It is an invitation from the greatest lover of all, our Bridegroom, Jesus. He is personally calling each of us to walk in deeper intimacy with Him. He not only offers us eternal life, but a divine relationship with Himself that is able to satisfy us above all else. In Psalm 63:3, David describes God's love as being 'better than life', meaning that in experiencing God's love He found something which was more valuable than anything this life could ever offer. Those who come to Him for Himself will never leave dissatisfied.

> Once we have tasted of the love of God, it is
> impossible to find our delight in anything but
> Himself.
>
> *Jeanne Marie Bouvier de la Motte-Guyon*[47]

When we have truly tasted and experienced God's love
it will reproduce a spiritual hunger in our hearts that will
leave us in pursuit of His presence. Those that come to
Him will never go away hungry, but at the same time will
live hungry for more of Him. If we come to Him with
agendas that do not seek to glorify Him, our hearts will
never truly be filled by Him. We will end up looking for
things elsewhere to fill a void that only Jesus can satisfy.

> Then Jesus declared, 'I am the bread of life.
> Whoever comes to me will never go hungry,
> and whoever believes in me will never be
> thirsty.'
> *John 6:35*

In the Gospel of John, Jesus refers to Himself as 'the
bread that comes down from heaven' (John 6:50). Jesus is
food for the hungry, and He is drink for the thirsty.[48] Only
He can truly fill the spiritual hunger deep within us and
nourish our souls. In order to sustain our physical bodies
and live a healthy life, we must have a good diet and eat
food which provides nourishment. It is the same in our
walk with God: in order to sustain a healthy relationship

---

[47] Jeanne Marie Bouvier de la Motte Guyon, *A Short Method of
Prayer.* (Peabody, MA: Hendrickson, 2006; first published in
1685), p 7 (Kindle edition), location 164.
[48] See John 7:37.

with Jesus and see our walk with Him deepen, we must continually come to Him and allow Him to feed us. Only Jesus is the true source of spiritual nourishment. To grow, we must come and feed on Him daily.[49] 'It is written: "Man shall not live on bread alone, but on every word that comes from the mouth of God"' (Matthew 4:4).

Coming to Jesus not only acknowledges our dependency upon His presence, it creates room for Him to speak to our hearts. Jesus is the living Word, as we read in John 1:14, and only through hearing His voice are we transformed. Jesus is not only revealed to us throughout the Scriptures, He is the One revealing the Scriptures to us, through His Spirit. As we take time to sit with Him in His presence, He is able to take the words from the pages of the Bible and write them upon our hearts.[50] We must take time to listen to Him, not just read for the sake of knowledge, but in our meditation upon His Word allow Him to kiss us through it. Only here can we be empowered to live a life obedient to the things He has spoken to us.

If you long in your heart to go deeper in your walk with Jesus, all you need to do is simply take time to be with Him. Jesus invites us to come and enter into His presence; it is the only place where our souls will ever truly find rest. It is here that God is able to lift the burdens of life which may weigh us down, and in return fill our hearts with joy and peace. It is in His presence that God empowers us with His Word so that He can bring to fruition all that He has purposed for our lives. As we live in Him, He lives through us. This is the continual invitation that Jesus

---

[49] See Matthew 6:11.
[50] See Hebrews 8:10; 10:16.

extends to us every day. Today and every day hereafter, may we continually hear His words reverberate in the depths of our hearts.

> Come to me, all you who are weary and burdened, and I will give you rest.
> *Matthew 11:28*

I knew what it meant to attend church on a Sunday. I was introduced to a religion, but I wasn't introduced to the person named Jesus, the One who passionately desired an intimate, loving relationship with me. Religion was never able to change me, nor was living by a set of rules or regulations. It was only the living presence and person of Jesus that was able to bring a genuine transformation on the inside and unveil truth to my heart.

Some of you may never have had a personal encounter with Jesus and if I ended this book without giving you the opportunity to meet Him personally for yourself, I would have missed giving you the greatest invitation that you will ever know.

We must understand, before ever making a commitment and decision to follow Jesus, that it was always God who chose to love us first.[51] Right from the beginning of creation, it was God's intention to live in an intimate relationship with us.[52] We were created by Him for this very purpose, in His image[53] and for His pleasure. However, humanity rebelled towards God, as we read in

---

[51] See 1 John 4:10.

[52] As we see in Genesis 3:8.

[53] See Genesis 1:27.

Genesis 3. So, humanity fell short of God's standard; we missed the mark and earned judgement.[54] This is where the root of our sinful nature is found, making us all imperfect and incomplete, separating us from the divine relationship humankind once had with God.

Thankfully God had a plan in place that would be able to restore our broken fellowship with Him once and for all. He came down to earth in the person of Jesus Christ. Fully man and fully God,[55] He lived a perfect and sinless life, a life that no man could ever live and yet humanity rejected Him and sentenced Him to death by crucifying Him. He was beaten so badly, to the point He became unrecognisable,[56] so that one day we might be recognised before God. Although Jesus was undeservedly sent to die on the cross, it was always God's ultimate plan to bring humanity back to Himself through the sacrifice of His Son, Jesus.

> For God so loved the world that he gave his one and only Son, that whoever believes in him shall not perish but have eternal life.
> John 3:16

Only Jesus, the perfect sacrifice, is able to remove the stain of sin upon our hearts and give us a new life. He took the penalty of our sin upon Himself so that we wouldn't have to be punished and sentenced to eternal death and separation from God.[57] Three days after He died, He rose

---

[54] See Romans 3:23.
[55] See Colossians 2:9.
[56] See Isaiah 52:14.
[57] See Romans 6:23.

from the grave, defeating death and fulfilling all Scripture, showing us that He truly is the Son of God. This is God's gift of salvation, not because it's what we deserve, but because of God's mercy and love for us. He invites us all to simply believe in what He accomplished on our behalf and in doing so we receive eternal life.

> If you declare with your mouth, 'Jesus is Lord,'
> and believe in your heart that God raised him
> from the dead, you will be saved.
> *Romans 10:9*

Only Jesus can fill the empty void that lies in every human heart. We are all in need of a saviour; in asking for His forgiveness and turning away from our sin, we cross over from death into life.[58] We become spiritually 'born again' as His children (John 3:3). He takes away our old life and in return gives us a new beginning. He revives every dead thing on the inside and causes us to spiritually come alive.

God not only makes us righteous, He empowers us to 'live righteous' for Him. When we surrender our hearts to Jesus, God the Holy Spirit comes and takes residence on the inside of us. The Holy Spirit is not something, He is someone, a real person that has feelings. He doesn't just give us new life; it is through Him and in Him that we can now live. The Holy Spirit is the One who leads us to look

---

[58] See John 5:24.

at Jesus,[59] and Jesus in return reveals the Father's heart: 'Anyone who has seen me has seen the Father' (John 14:9).

Whatever your current situation may be, today, Jesus is personally inviting each of you to come to Him and receive the gift of eternal life. He is calling you back to Himself. In responding to His invitation, I encourage you to read this short prayer aloud from your heart. Spend some time simply fixing your inward gaze towards Him and let Him touch you with His love:

> Precious Lord Jesus, today I come to You, empty and broken, and as one who has sinned against You. Today I ask You for Your forgiveness. I believe that You are the Son of God, who came down to earth and died for my sins and on the third day You rose again. Wash me and cleanse me with Your blood, set me free and make me new. Today I turn from my sin and look to You as my Lord and Saviour. I surrender my life to You and receive Your gift of eternal life. Thank You, Jesus, for what You have done for me. Fill me with Your Holy Spirit and guide me all the days of my life. From today onwards I am Yours and You are mine. I love You. Amen.

> Therefore, if anyone is in Christ, the new creation has come: the old has gone, the new is here!
> *2 Corinthians 5:17*

---

[59] John 16:5-15 tells us something of the Spirit's work. See also 1 Corinthians 2:10.

It gives me great joy that I am able to rejoice in what Jesus has done for you. This is the beginning of your beautiful, unique journey with God. It may start today with a prayer, but it is sustained as you follow Him daily. If you have given your heart to Jesus, or have recommitted your life to Him, I encourage you to continually seek His face and spend time with Him. God will never leave nor forsake you, as He promises in Hebrews 13:5. If you haven't already got one, get a modern translation of the Bible,[60] and begin to spend time reading it. Ask Jesus to unveil His word to your heart. If another believer gave you this book, please share with them the wonderful decision you have made to follow Jesus. I also encourage you to pray and ask God to lead you to a loving local church, one where they teach the Bible and welcome God's presence. It is God's heart that we do not walk this journey alone;[61] He gives us a kingdom family in which we can grow, encourage one another and remain accountable.

In every season we go through in life, whether on the mountaintop or down in the valley below, God has promised to be with us on the journey. Place your trust in Him alone and know that His goodness never changes. He will never fail to satisfy you.

Lastly, my prayer is that you may continually find rest at the feet of Jesus, and above all enjoy all that He is.

---

[60] Such as the NIV.

[61] In Hebrews 10:25 we are exhorted not to stop 'meeting together'.

Contact

To find out more about David and Noreen's ministry, visit the Kingdom Encounter website at:
www.kingdomencounter.com

or email:
info@kingdomencounter.com